SCHOLASTIC

44 Book

Photo: Ken Karp
Illustrations: © Bill Greenhead and Tim Haggerty
pp. 182–183: Animated Speech Corporation

Copyright © 2009 by Scholastic Inc.

ISBN-13: 978-0-439-74159-0
ISBN-10: 0-439-74159-9

3 4 5 6 7 8 9 10   31   17 16 15 14 13 12 11 10 09 08

 **Printed on recycled paper.**

Table of Contents

Table of Contents continued

Table of Contents continued

To the teacher:

An Answer Key is available on SAM.
SAM Keyword: 44Book Answers

SCHOLASTIC

SYSTEM 44

Dear *System 44* Student,

Welcome to the *44Book*! This is where you can practice using the skills and strategies you've been learning in *System 44*.

How to Find the Right Practice Pages

You can find the page that goes with any software Topic by looking at the Topic number printed at the top or in the table of contents. Your teacher may also assign pages to go with lessons.

Using the *System 44* Handbook

The Handbook section at the back is a place you can turn to for help. Use the Glossary to look up or review terms used in *System 44* instruction. You can use the Software and Reading logs to keep track of the software Topics you finish and books you read. There are also other reference pages that can help.

Getting the Most from Your *44Book*

- **Use the Review boxes.** Read the text in the Review boxes to study important skills and concepts you're working on.

- **Follow the instructions.** Be sure you understand the instructions for each activity before you begin. Ask a teacher, partner, or family member for help in understanding the instructions when you need to.

- **Work with a partner.** Take turns completing activities. Talk with each other about how you figured out each answer.

Keep on learning!

Ivan

Name _____

Write It

▶ **A.** Write an *m* under the pictures whose names begin with *m*.

1.

_____ _____ _____

2.

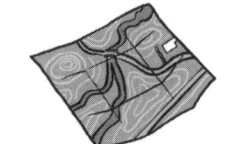 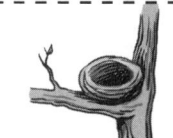 

_____ _____ _____

▶ **B.** Write an *s* under the pictures whose names begin with *s*.

3.

_____ _____ _____

4.

_____ _____ _____

Review

- Consonant *m* stands for the sound you hear at the beginning of the word *map* and at the end of the word *jam*.
- Consonant *s* stands for the sound you hear at the beginning of the word *sun*.

 Use with **Teaching Guide,** *page 106.*

Spelling Pattern

t as in *top*,
n as in *net*

Name

Write It

▶ **A.** Write a *t* under the pictures whose names begin with *t*.

1.

_____ _____ _____

2.

_____ _____ _____

▶ **B.** Write an *n* under the pictures whose names begin with *n*.

3.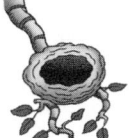

_____ _____ _____

4.

_____ _____ _____

Review

- Consonant *t* stands for the sound you hear at the beginning of the word *top* and at the end of the word *hat*.
- Consonant *n* stands for the sound you hear at the beginning of the word *net* and at the end of the word *pan*.

*Use with **Teaching Guide**, page 110.*

Name

Word List

▶ Read the words from left to right. Then, circle any three words with a consonant-vowel-consonant pattern (**CVC**).

an	at	man	mat	sat	am	tan	mat	an	tan	sat
at	an	man	sat	am	tan	man				

Puzzle Fun

▶ Use words from the word bank to fill in the puzzle. Some letters are filled in for you.

an	at	man
mat	sat	tan

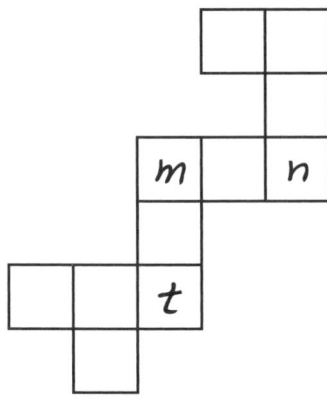

Name

Word List

▶ Read the words from left to right. Then, circle the words that begin with *p* as in ***pan***. Underline the words that begin with *c* as in *cat*.

| can mat man cap cat am an nap map tap sat |
| at pan man sat cat pat sap |

Review

pan

cat

- Consonant *p* stands for the sound you hear at the beginning of the word *pan*.
- Consonant *c* can stand for the sound you hear at the beginning of the word *cat*.

Rhyme It

▶ Read each word in the word bank. Then, find four rhyming words for each word listed below. The first one is started for you.

map	cat	pan	nap	tan
mat	pat	tap	sat	sap
can	man			

1. an   _pan_   _tan_   _____   _____

2. at   _____   _____   _____   _____

3. cap   _____   _____   _____   _____

Use with **Teaching Guide**, *page 124.*

b as in *bat*, *r* as in *ran*

Name

Review

bat

ran

- Consonant *b* stands for the sound you hear at the beginning of the word *bat*.
- Consonant *r* stands for the sound you hear at the beginning of the word *ran*.

Word List

▶ Read the words from left to right. Then, circle the words that begin with *b* as in *bat*. Underline the words that begin with *r* as in *ran*.

bat	cap	ram	rat	tan	rap	cab	bat	can	rap	sat
ban	ran	ram	pat	ban	ran	cab				

Write It

▶ Write the correct word from the word bank next to each picture.

bat	can	cab	cat	pan	map

1. _____

4. _____

2. _____

5. _____

3. _____

6. _____

 Use with **Teaching Guide**, *page 128.*

Sight Words | Name _____

Word List

▶ Read the words from left to right. Then, circle the words you think you have used today.

| are | the | are | has | he | a | has | this | my | this | this |
| the | is | my | you | a | I | he | | | | |

Sentence Solver

▶ Use words from the word bank to complete each sentence.

| are | my | he |
| is | I | has |

1. _____ am sad.

2. Mom _____ a pet cat.

3. Cam and Sam _____ mad.

4. _____ dad can rap.

5. The cap _____ tan.

6. _____ is at bat.

Use with **Teaching Guide,** page 524.

Name

Word List

► Read the words from left to right. Then, circle the words with an **-s ending.**

cans	tab	bats	map	pats	naps	raps	cabs	bat
pat	rams	caps	pans	nap	cat	mats	can	cap

Sentence Solver

► **A.** Use words from the word bank to complete each sentence.

naps	bats	cats

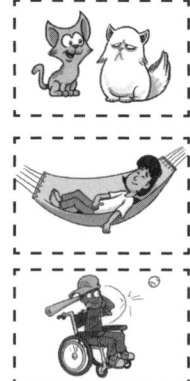

1. He pats the _____.

2. Pam _____.

3. Cam _____.

Mark It

► **B.** Underline each base word and circle each word ending. The first one is done for you.

4. pat(s)

5. naps

6. bats

Use with **Teaching Guide,** page 132.

Review

I have six caps.

He pats the cat.

- An **ending** can be added to a base word.
- The **-s ending** on naming words, or nouns, tells that there is more than one of something.
- The **-s ending** is also used on action words, or verbs, in some sentences.

Series 1 Review · Name

Word List

▶ Read the words from left to right. The words are new, but you have the skills to read them. Circle the words with an *-s* ending.

| as | bans | rats | tab | tabs | tans | tap |

<table>
<tr><td colspan="2">**Series 1 Review**</td></tr>
<tr><td>1.3</td><td>man, tan</td></tr>
<tr><td>1.4</td><td>pan, cat</td></tr>
<tr><td>1.5</td><td>bat, ran</td></tr>
<tr><td>1.6</td><td>sight words</td></tr>
<tr><td>1.7</td><td>caps, pats</td></tr>
</table>

Word Search

▶ Circle the words. The words can be down or across.

bat	caps	cats
raps	this	tab
tabs	the	my

c	n	s	p	m	g	q	e	l	r	c	k
a	f	r	w	t	t	a	b	i	q	j	e
p	y	c	f	r	m	r	e	b	a	t	b
s	t	h	e	s	b	s	l	u	p	c	p
g	u	w	q	j	k	z	w	z	y	a	i
t	z	i	n	r	a	p	s	t	k	t	q
a	z	s	p	a	q	a	z	w	n	s	c
b	h	p	z	q	k	u	c	y	q	x	o
s	q	a	t	h	i	s	o	i	w	m	y

Just for Fun

▶ Say this tongue twister five times fast!

Can cats nap? Cats can nap! Cats nap!

 *Use with **Teaching Guide,** page 542.*

Name _____

Word List

▶ Read the words from left to right. Then, circle the words with **short *i*** as in *rip*.

| in pin pan sip tan bit it rap taps tin sit sat |
| sap rim mats bat tip rip |

Sentence Solver

▶ Use words from the word bank to complete each sentence. Use the pictures to help you. The first one is done for you.

| sip | rim | rip | sit | bit | pin |

1. It hit the ___rim___.

2. Pam has a _____. It has a map on it.

3. My cap has a _____.

4. I _____ in the cab.

5. Tim _____ into the ribs.

6. I can _____ from the tap.

*Use with **Teaching Guide**, page 140.*

d as in *dog*, *f* as in *fan*

Name _____

Word List

▶ Read the words from left to right. Then, circle the words that begin with *d* as in *dog*. Underline the words that begin with *f* as in *fan*.

fan	sit	dim	rid	fin	dip	ran	rim	bat	fad	mats
in	mad	bad	sad	fit	sip	tip				

Review

dog

fan

- Consonant *d* stands for the sound you hear at the beginning of the word *dog*.

- Consonant *f* stands for the sound you hear at the beginning of the word *fan*.

All Mixed Up

▶ Unscramble the sentences. Write them on the line.

1. bit I bad rib a _____.

2. sad not Dad is _____.

3. has pan lid The a _____.

4. pan in fits the It _____.

5. cat My fat is _____.

6. tip fan The can _____.

 *Use with **Teaching Guide**, page 144.*

Spelling Pattern

h as in *hat*, *k* as in *kid*   **Name** _____

Word List

▶ Read the words from left to right. Then, circle the words that begin with *h* as in *hat*. Underline the words that begin with *k* as in *kid*.

| dim | hat | rid | had | fin | kit | hip | ram | maps | tip | him |

kid ham bad hit hid kin cabs

Math Facts

▶ Change the letters to spell new words. Then, write the words on the lines to make a sentence. The first one is done for you.

1. bid – b + h = _hid_   ham – m + t = _hat_

   Kit _hid_ my _hat_.

2. pad – p + h = _____   hat – h + f = _____   fat – f + c = _____

   Kim _____ a _____ _____.

3. mat – t + n = _____   tap – p + n = _____   can – n + p = _____

   The _____ has a _____ _____.

4. in – n + s = _____   hit – i + a = _____

   This _____ my _____.

5. kit – t + d = _____   mat – t + p = _____

   This _____ has a _____.

*Use with **Teaching Guide**, page 148.*

Name

Review

h<u>o</u>t

m<u>o</u>p

These words have the **short *o* vowel sound**. Letter *o* usually stands for the **short *o*** sound in words with a consonant-vowel-consonant pattern **(CVC)**.

Word List

▶ Read the words from left to right. Then, put a star by the words with **short *o*** as in *h<u>o</u>t*.

hop	cats	top	hip	kit	pit	sob	mats	not	pop
map	dot	tip	tap	pot	nod	mop	mom		

Puzzle Fun

▶ Use the word bank to fill in the puzzle. One is done for you.

dot	pot	top	mop
stop	sob	cob	cot

Across

2.

5.

6.

Down

1.

2.

3.

4.

5.

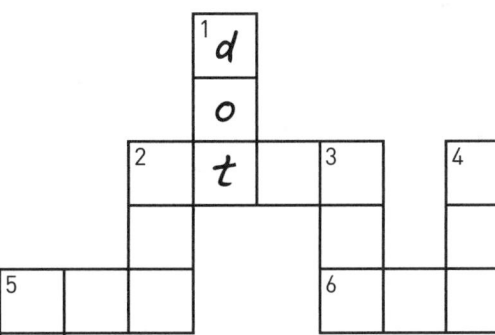

Use with **Teaching Guide,** *page 152.*

l as in *lips, x* as in *box*

Name _____

Review

lips

box

- Consonant *l* stands for the sound you hear at the beginning of the word *lips*.
- Consonant *x* stands for the sound you hear at the end of the word *box*.

Word List

▶ Read the words from left to right. Then, circle the words that begin with *l* as in *lips*. Underline the words that end with *x* as in *box*.

lab	fox	lot	mom	tip	lips	lit	box	pot	six	hot
lap	sit	fit	mix	fix	tab	cans			

Chain Letters

▶ Change one letter in each word to make a new word. Use words from the word bank. You will use some words more than once. The first one is done for you.

tap	cat	tip	six
lip	top	fit	pot
tan	rip	fin	sip
mix	fix	lap	map

1. box → _fox_ → fix

2. fix → _____ → tin → _____ → tap → _____ → sip

3. hat → _____ → can → _____ → tap → _____ → mop

4. mix → _____ → fin → _____ → lit → _____ → lap →
   sap → _____ → tip

5. mix → _____ → sip → _____ → top → pop → _____ → hot

Name _____

Review

lo<u>ck</u>

ti<u>ck</u>

The letters *-ck* stand for the sound you hear at the end of these words.

Word List

▶ Read the words from left to right. Then, circle the words that end with *-ck* as in *lo<u>ck</u>*.

back	sick	tick	kit	kick	bad	tip	pack	pick	lips
six	lock	pit	sack	fix	sock	box	rock		

Word Search

▶ **A.** Circle the words. The words can be down or across.

box	lock	dock	pack
fox	sack	fix	dim

t i c k p a c k

d l o c k f o x

o t o c k d i m

c f i x s a c k

k b o x r o c k

▶ **B.** Use the remaining letters to find the answer to the question, **"What music do clocks like to play?"** Write the answer on the line below.

_____

Sight Words

Name _____

Word List

▶ Read the words from left to right. Then, circle the words that you think are most difficult to spell.

> a is me are my that do I has she of to and
> he they look the what

Word Hunt

▶ Fill in the missing word in each sentence. The first one is done for you.

1. I had a lot __*of*__ ham.
   - **a.** if
   - **b.** of
   - **c.** at

2. Mom _____ I pat the cat.
   - **a.** and
   - **b.** him
   - **c.** am

3. Can you fix _____ fan?
   - **a.** him
   - **b.** lid
   - **c.** that

4. _____ did Mom pack in the box?
   - **a.** What
   - **b.** Not
   - **c.** Can

5. _____ at the fox!
   - **a.** Let
   - **b.** Lock
   - **c.** Look

6. _____ had six pets.
   - **a.** The
   - **b.** They
   - **c.** That

*Use with **Teaching Guide**, page 524.*

Name _____

Word List

▶ Read the words from left to right. The words are new, but you have the skills to read them. Circle the words with **short o** as in *hot*.

Series 2 Review	
2.1	rip , pin
2.2	dog, fan
2.3	hat, kid
2.4	hot, mop
2.5	lips, box
2.6	lock, tick
2.7	sight words

dad   did   hops   pots   tax   packs   rack
tacks   fax   pins

Sentence Solver

Use words from the word bank to complete each sentence. The first one is done for you.

look	sob	ham	back	do
fix	kit	hip	fan	

1. Kim had a bit of __ham__.

2. Mom has pins in this _____.

3. Jen and Dan _____ not run in the lab.

4. Can you _____ my sock? It has a rip.

5. I am not a rock _____.

6. If Lim is sad, he will _____.

7. He has a bad _____ and _____.

8. Did you _____ in the box?

Use with **Teaching Guide**, *page 542*.

Name

Word List

▶ Read the words from left to right. Then, circle the words with *s*-blends.

| stick | sick | spin | stack | hot | sack | spot | slam | sock |
| him | stop | tick | cap | span | slap | slid | sat | slim |

Review

slim

spin

stop

Letter *s* often appears with other consonants to form **consonant blends**. The letters in a consonant blend go together, but you can hear the sound each consonant stands for.

Sort It

▶ Read the words in the word bank. Then, write each one under the word that begins with the same consonant blend.

| slick | stock | slip | span | stick |
| slap | stack | slim | spin | slid |

1. s̲lam	2. s̲pot	3. s̲top

Use with **Teaching Guide,** *page 166.*

Name

Word List

► Read the words from left to right. Then, circle the words with the **short _e_ sound** you hear in _set_.

men	sled	bat	pen	fad	stem	man	neck	stop
speck	pat	step	bed	dim	dock	pet	deck	bad

Review

set

stem

These words have the **short _e_ vowel sound.** Letter _e_ usually stands for the short _e_ sound in words with a consonant-vowel-consonant pattern (**CVC**).

Find It

► Read each clue. Write the word from the word bank that goes with each clue. The first one is done for you.

bed	step	men	stem
sled	pet	speck	ten

1. You can slip down a hill with me. _____sled_____

2. I am 5 + 5. _____

3. I am a cat. _____

4. You can rest on me. _____

5. I am not 1 man, but 2. _____

6. I am a part of a plant. _____

7. I am just a bit. _____

8. I can help you get up to the deck. _____

 *Use with **Teaching Guide**, page 170.*

Name _____

Word List

▶ Read the words from left to right. Then, circle the words with *j* as in *jet*. Underline the words with *w* as in <u>*win*</u>.

wick	pick	jet	web	net	wet	ram	jam	tax
wax	sled	led	wed	tin	hot	jot	win	job

Sentence Solver

▶ Use words from the word bank to complete each sentence.

jam	jet	wet	jot	win

1. Kim went on a trip in a _____.

2. Sam will _____ the top spot.

3. The cat fell in the tub and is _____.

4. Jim has _____ on a bun for a snack.

5. Get a pen and _____ this on a pad.

Write It

▶ Choose a word from the word bank. Use it in a sentence.

6. _____

Use with **Teaching Guide,** *page 174.*

Spelling Pattern

Short *u* as in *up*

Name

Word List

▶ Read the words from left to right. Then, circle the words with the **short *u* sound** you hear in *up*.

mud	cut	bat	stuck	deck	lack	run	mom	up
luck	rib	ham	bus	slam	rub	hum	stick	duck

Write It

▶ Say the name of each picture. Write the name of the picture on the line.

1.

_____

4.

_____

7.

_____

2.

_____

5.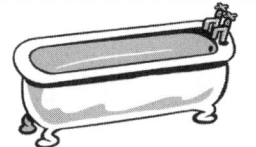

_____

8.

_____

3.

_____

6.

_____

9.

_____

 Use with **Teaching Guide,** *page 178.*

Spelling Pattern

g as in *gas*, *y* as in *yuck*

Name

Review

gas

yuck

- Consonant *g* can stand for the sound you hear at the beginning of the word *gas*.
- Consonant *y* can stand for the sound you hear at the beginning of the word *yuck*.

Word List

▶ Read the words from left to right. Then, circle the words with *g* as in *gas*. Underline the words with *y* as in *yuck*.

dig	dim	gas	luck	yuck	bug	bun	job	yet	bet
jog	yes	ham	yam	big	tip	rug	run		

Circle It

▶ Read each clue. Then, circle the correct word.

1. This can be a snack.   yam   yes
2. A dog can do this.   wig   wag
3. A web can trap this.   yes   bug
4. You can stand on this.   rug   dig
5. The snack is bad.   get   yuck

Complete It

▶ Complete each word by filling in the blank with *y* or *g*. You may use a dictionary for help.

6. di _____

7. _____ uck

8. _____ es

9. bi _____

10. _____ as

Use with **Teaching Guide,** *page 184.*

Name

Word List

▶ Read the words from left to right. Then, circle the words with **q** as in **quiz**. Underline the words with **v** as in **van** and put a star by the words that start with **z** as in **zip**.

| quit van zip hip quick wick quack slam vet yet |
| spin sock quiz vat zag jog rap zap |

Link It

▶ **A.** Finish each word chain. Add or change one letter at a time. Some are done for you.

1. Go from **yes** to **vet**.

yes
yet
vet

2. Go from **rap** to **zip**.

_____
_____
zip

3. Go from **mat** to **van**.

mat
_____
_____

▶ **B.** Read each item. Write your answer on the line.

4. Change just one letter of **quack** to make a new word.

_____

5. Write a word that rhymes with **zap.**

_____

Review

van
quiz
zip

- Consonant **v** stands for the sound you hear at the beginning of the word **van**.
- Consonant **q** always appears with the letter **u** and stands for the sound you hear at the beginning of the word **quiz**.
- Consonant **z** stands for the sound you hear at the beginning of the word **zip**.

*Use with **Teaching Guide,** page 188.*

Name

Word List

▶ Read the words from left to right. Then, circle the words you think you have used today.

for	are	said	of	by	like	the	her	no	has	they
look	have	what	you	will	with	from				

Sentence Solver

▶ Use words from the word bank to complete each sentence. The first one is done for you.

will	from	with
said	no	have

1. Do you ___*have*___ a red cap?

2. I jog _____ my dad.

3. The dog got a snack _____ the vet.

4. Ms. Tan _____ to pick up the pens.

5. _____ Max pack his bag?

6. I am mad. I just have _____ luck!

*Use with **Teaching Guide**, page 524.*

Series 3 Review

Name _____

Word List

▶ Read the words from left to right. The words are new, but you have the skills to read them. Circle the words with **s-blends**.

cup	fun	pens	slot	suds	fog	hen	pigs
steps	sun							

Series 3 Review	
3.1	slim, spin, stop
3.2	set, stem
3.3	jet, win
3.4	up, luck
3.5	gas, yuck
3.6	van, quiz, zip
3.7	sight words

All Mixed Up

▶ **A.** Unscramble each word to match a word in the word bank. The first one is done for you.

jet	slip	gap	vet	stuck
quit	her	from	bun	

1. nbu   _b_ _u_ _n_
                 6   7

2. ehr   __ __ __
             1

3. vte   __ __ __
             3

4. tcusk   __ __ __ __ __
               10

5. rofm   __ __ __ __
              5

6. pga   __ __ __
                 2

7. plsi   __ __ __ __
                      8

8. etj   __ __ __
                 4

9. tqiu   __ __ __ __
                      9

▶ **B.** Write each numbered letter from above on the lines below that have the same number. Then, read the secret message.

10. __ __ __ __   __ __ __   __ __
        1   2   3   4   5   6   7   8   7

__ __ __   __ __ __!
9   1   4   10   6   7

*Use with **Teaching Guide,** page 542.*

s-Blends

Name _____

Word List

▶ Read the words from left to right. Then, circle the words with *sc* as in *scam*. Underline the words with *sk* as in *skid*. Put a star by the words with *sn* as in *snip*.

skip	scab	pans	skim	ban	slid	yes	snap	scan
quiz	stick	skid	dim	skit	snug	stop	snack	snip

Build It

▶ Build at least six words using one letter or letter pair from each box. One is done for you. Use a dictionary to check your work.

Beginning Letters	Vowels	Ending Letters
sn sk sc	a i	b m n p t

1. _____scan_____   4. _____

2. _____   5. _____

3. _____   6. _____

Bonus Can you build any more words?

7. _____   8. _____

Double Consonants as in *sniff*, *skull*, and *mess*

Name

Word List

▶ Read the words from left to right. Then, circle the words that end with two of the same consonants.

stuff	stock	spell	quick	kiss	skull	spin	sniff	cuff
men	sell	kid	skit	skill	mess	snack	sick	spill

Review

sniff

skull

mess

When two of the same consonants appear together, they usually stand for one sound.

Replace It

▶ Replace the underlined letter or letters with **ff**, **ll**, or **ss** to make a new word. The first one is done for you.

ff	ll	ss

1. wic<u>k</u> _____*will*_____

2. pa<u>n</u> _____

3. set<u>s</u> _____

4. le<u>t</u> _____

5. stu<u>b</u> _____

6. spec<u>k</u> _____

7. spi<u>n</u> _____

8. ski<u>m</u> _____

9. me<u>t</u> _____

10. sni<u>p</u> _____

*Use with **Teaching Guide,** page 196.*

Name

Word List

▶ Read the words from left to right. Then, circle the words that end with an **s-blend**.

lips	**desk**	**list**	**rest**	**fast**	**spill**	**dust**	**snug**	**best**
beds	**risk**	**step**	**ask**	**deck**	**test**	**quick**	**mask**	**mats**

Word Search

▶ Circle the words. The words can be down or across.

risk	**neck**	**ask**	**west**
mask	**nest**	**fast**	**rest**

```
f  u  b  r  z  d  y  r  q  c  k
a  l  q  w  j  r  q  e  z  j  e
s  j  n  e  c  k  m  s  b  y  b
t  m  a  s  k  w  z  t  p  q  p
j  z  o  t  q  n  b  z  y  a  i
q  a  r  d  w  e  n  l  k  s  q
z  s  j  r  i  s  k  m  n  l  c
u  k  q  w  c  t  h  z  w  m  y
```

Review

risk

fast

Letter **s** often appears with other consonants to form **consonant blends**. The letters in a consonant blend go together, but you can hear the sound each consonant stands for.

*Use with **Teaching Guide**, page 200.*

Identifying Syllables

Name _____

Word List

▶ Read the words from left to right. Then, circle the words with two syllables.

seven	snack	contest	skill	tennis	lock	denim
skim	magnet	basket	laptop	ask	dentist	test
desk	disgust	mask	muffin			

> ### Review
>
> A useful strategy for reading words with more than one syllable is to:
> - **Spot** the vowels to identify the number of syllables.
> - **Split** the word into syllables.
> - **Read** each part and then read the whole word.

Split It

▶ Circle the vowel spots in each word. Then, draw a line to split the words into syllables. Write the syllables on the lines. The first one is done for you.

1. d(e)n|t(i)st   _den_   _tist_

2. contest   _____ _____

3. laptop   _____ _____

4. rabbit   _____ _____

5. seven   _____ _____

6. magnet   _____ _____

7. tennis   _____ _____

8. baskets   _____ _____

9. muffin   _____ _____

10. insist   _____ _____

Sight Words Name

Word List

► Read the words from left to right. Then, circle the words that you think are the most difficult to spell.

| was by for go from out good have very talk |
| some who her so they call look what |

Sentence Solver

► **A.** Use words from the word bank to complete each sentence.

| very | talk | good | was |
| out | who | some | call |

1. _____ Jim at camp?

2. I am _____ glad that Grant is my pal.

3. _____ will win the contest?

4. A muffin is a _____ snack.

5. Did you _____ Ms. Lam?

6. _____ dogs can run fast.

► **B.** Find the words from the word bank that you did not use. Use each one in a sentence.

7. _____

8. _____

Name

Series 4 Review	
4.1	<u>scam</u>, <u>skid</u>, <u>snip</u>
4.2	<u>sniff</u>, <u>skull</u>, <u>mess</u>
4.3	<u>risk</u>, <u>fast</u>
4.4	con|test, lap|top
4.5	sight words

Word List

▶ Read the words from left to right. The words are new, but you have the skills to read them. Circle the words with two syllables.

> pass   rests   skips   spills   fell   yell   disk   gossip
> sunset   upset

Puzzle Fun

▶ Fill in the crossword puzzle with words from the word bank.

> brisk   skills   tennis   talk
> sell   was   pass

Across

1. *is*, in the past

3. fast

4. If you do well on a test, you do this.

6. chat

Down

2. If you are good at something, you have these.

5. Shops do this.

6. You can play a match of this game.

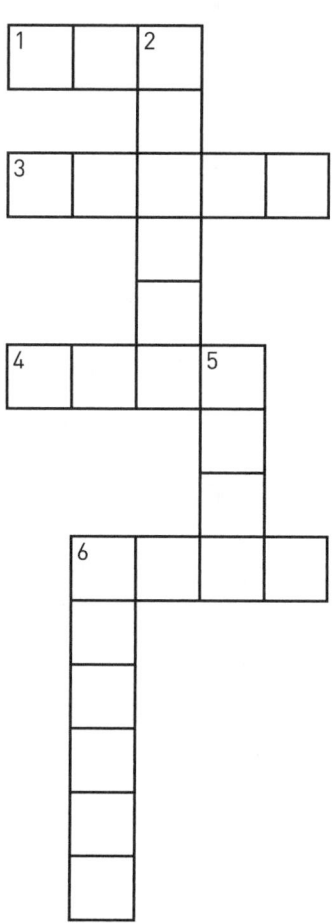

Spelling Pattern
l-Blends

Name _____

Word List

▶ Read the words from left to right. Then, circle the words with **l-blends**.

> cliff sniff clock click clap pack laptop black
> glad kick stock club snap blog magnet insist
> block glass

Review

black
club
glad

Letter *l* often appears with other consonants to form **consonant blends**. The letters in a consonant blend go together, but you can hear the sound each consonant stands for.

Link It

▶ **A.** Finish each word chain. Add or change one letter at a time. The first one is done for you.

1. Go from **hop** to **blog**.	2. Go from **tip** to **clap**.	3. Go from **sick** to **block**.
hop	tip	sick
hog	tap	
log		lock
blog		

▶ **B.** Read each item. Write your answer on the blank.

4. Add one letter to the beginning of **lip** to make a new word.

_____

5. Add one letter to the beginning of **lad** to make a new word.

_____

Name _____

Word List

► Read the words from left to right. Then, circle the words with *r*-blends.

crust	crop	fast	frost	class	blog	frog	brim	skim
crab	cross	brag	rust	skill	blast	brick	scab	brass

All Mixed Up

► Unscramble the words to complete each sentence.

fret	brim	crop	frog	brag
crib	bricks	frost	brass	crab

1. The trumpet is _____. **sabrs**

2. A _____ has legs and a shell. **abcr**

3. A _____ hops and likes to get wet. **rfgo**

4. Fill the milk to the _____ of the glass. **mbir**

5. They will _____ if they do well on the test. **grba**

6. Do not _____! It will be OK! **erft**

7. Tran will plant the _____. **proc**

8. There is _____ on the grass. **rfsto**

9. The cabin is made of logs, not _____. **kcrisb**

10. My sis is in her _____. **ricb**

*Use with **Teaching Guide**, page 218.*

Name

Word List

▶ Read the words from left to right. Then, circle the words with *l-blends*. Underline the words with *r-blends*.

brass grass black flip stack brag flag plan trust
desk plus crust plot track best drop stop truck

Puzzle Fun

▶ Use words from the word bank to fill in the puzzle. The first one is done for you.

plum	truck	plus	trust
flag	grass	drag	track

Across

2. I run on the ____.

4. Ten ____ ten is twenty.

5. My dad cuts the ____.

6. Fran has a pickup ____.

Down

1. A ____ can be made of fabric.

2. I can ____ my mom.

3. I cannot lift this, so I will ____ it.

4. A ____ is a good snack.

Name _____

Word List

▶ Read the words from left to right. Then, circle the words that begin with **two-letter blends.** Underline the words that begin with **three-letter blends.**

luck	laptop	lips	split	struck	laps	sprint	scrap
insist	strip	strap	twist	list	swim	denim	less
stress	strum						

> ### Review
>
> <u>tw</u>in
>
> <u>scr</u>ub
>
> <u>spr</u>int
>
> **Consonant blends** may be made up of two or three consonants together.

Sentence Solver

▶ Use words from the word bank to complete each sentence.

twin	strap	swim
sprint	split	scrub

1. A _____ is a quick run.

2. Brock will _____ the snack. I will have a bit, and he will have a bit!

3. I will have to _____ my pants to get the mud out.

4. I have a _____. He is just like me!

5. Quin has a _____ on his bag.

6. If it is hot out, we can _____.

Use with **Teaching Guide,** page 222.

Sight Words Name

Word List

▶ Read the words from left to right. Then, circle the words you think you have used today.

> your very friend was already we who be so
> live with two said no there what one see

Word Hunt

▶ Fill in the missing word in each sentence.

1. Did you _____ the film?
 a. six
 b. see
 c. set

2. My _____ Cris is in my class.
 a. friend
 b. from
 c. frost

3. _____ is a muffin on her desk.
 a. They
 b. The
 c. There

4. Brad and Greg _____ on my block.
 a. live
 b. lint
 c. like

5. I _____ had a snack.
 a. and
 b. are
 c. already

6. _____ had fun with the kitten.
 a. We
 b. With
 c. Win

7. Is this _____ laptop?
 a. you
 b. your
 c. yet

8. Five plus _____ is six.
 a. on
 b. out
 c. one

9. Will Jess _____ at the club?
 a. be
 b. best
 c. ban

10. Liz has _____ dogs.
 a. to
 b. two
 c. tip

Series 5 Review   Name

Series 5 Review	
5.1	<u>bl</u>ack, <u>cl</u>ub, <u>gl</u>ad
5.2	<u>br</u>im, <u>cr</u>ab, <u>fr</u>ost
5.3	<u>fl</u>at, <u>tr</u>ack
5.4	<u>tw</u>in, <u>scr</u>ub, <u>spr</u>int
5.5	sight words

Word List

▶ Read the words from left to right. The words are new, but you have the skills to read them. Circle the word with a **three-letter blend**.

crusts	fled	straps	trap	drills	clips	flex	grid
trick	dress						

Word Search

▶ Circle the words. The words can be down, across, or diagonal.

clips	crusts	there	fled	grid
trap	drills	snaps	less	stick

c	p	q	s	z	d	l	e	s	s	f
t	r	w	r	t	e	r	z	s	p	l
r	l	u	e	q	i	y	i	w	d	e
a	w	z	s	s	d	c	z	l	q	d
p	d	c	e	t	j	n	k	m	l	s
e	s	n	a	p	s	l	w	x	j	s
v	b	z	y	y	p	g	r	i	d	g
c	l	i	p	s	g	s	q	t	e	z
o	u	d	z	q	f	t	h	e	r	e

 *Use with **Teaching Guide**, page 542.*

Name _____

Word List

▶ Read the words from left to right. Then, circle the words that end with a **consonant blend.**

> gift   stamp   jump   less   left   raft   fans   fact   at   act
> scrap   slam   strum   split   help   lift   camp   lick

Puzzle Fun

▶ Use words from the word bank to fill in the puzzle.

lamp	raft	jump	left	stamp
act	fact	gift	lift	help

Across

3. Stick this on a note that you want to send.

5. This is the opposite of right.

8. You can drift on this.

9. I just fell! Can you ___ me up?

Down

1. My pal sent me a ___ on my birthday.

2. I like to ___ rope.

4. Mick will ___ in the class play.

5. That box is big, but Max can ___ it!

6. 10 + 10 = 20 is a ___.

7. Can you see? Switch on the ___.

 *Use with **Teaching Guide**, page 200.*

-nk as in *blink*,
ng as in *wing*

Name _____

Word List

▶ Read the words from left to right. Then, circle the words that end in blend **-nk**. Underline the words that end in digraph **ng**.

drink	link	blanket	song	skunk	back	junk	wins
bank	seven	wing	lick	stung	struck	king	split
kiss	ring						

All Mixed Up

▶ **A.** Unscramble each of the words from the word bank.

king	skunk	song	bring	bank	stung

1. nkba _____

3. osng _____

5. ribgn _____

2. ingk _____

4. ngust _____

6. suknk _____

▶ **B.** Circle the words from the word bank. The words can be down, across, or diagonal.

k	b	d	q	t	s	v	u
s	s	o	n	g	k	a	q
v	t	e	e	i	u	z	c
k	i	u	f	j	n	p	k
i	d	s	n	j	k	k	b
n	w	s	c	g	b	v	a
g	t	b	r	i	n	g	n
h	z	q	n	w	x	z	k

*Use with **Teaching Guide,** page 200.*

Closed Syllables

Name _____

Word List

▶ Read the words from left to right. Then, circle the words with **two syllables**.

> plastic   blink   fantastic   hundred   jacket   stack   draft
>
> pocket   traffic   planet   stung   drastic   king   plans
>
> fans   habit   facts   limit

Split It

▶ **A.** Circle the vowel spots in each word. Then, draw a line to split the words into syllables. Write the syllables on the lines. The first one is done for you.

1. p(i)c|n(i)c _pic_   _nic_

2. traffic _____ _____

3. rapid _____ _____

4. jacket _____ _____

5. ticket _____ _____

6. drastic _____ _____

7. plastic _____ _____

8. fantastic _____ _____ _____

9. hundred _____ _____

10. limit _____ _____

▶ **B.** Choose two words from above and use each one in a sentence.

11. _____

12. _____

*Use with **Teaching Guide,** page 208.*

Spelling Pattern

Ending Blends   Name

Word List

▶ Read the words from left to right. Then, circle the words that end with **-nd**. Underline the words that end with **-nt**.

pond	send	camp	scrap	band	bank	strand	strap
plant	stamp	stand	staff	tent	wing	blend	sand
miss	mint						

Sentence Solver

▶ Use words from the word bank to complete each sentence.

blend	pond	hint	send	plant
stand	band	tent	mint	sand

1. Do not _____ in the street.

2. Did you see that fish jump in the _____?

3. The truck got stuck in the _____.

4. At camp, we slept in a big _____.

5. If you _____ the crops in spring, you will have them in the fall.

6. Dad will _____ the milk and eggs.

7. I like drinks that have _____.

8. Min will stamp the letter and _____ it to you.

9. What is in the box? Tell me a _____!

10. Jeff has to get drums for his _____.

 Use with Teaching Guide, page 200.

Sight Words   Name _____

Word List

▶ Read the words from left to right. Then, circle the words you think you have used today.

> or were came friend one now make there
> two your already give very use come goes
> who ahead

Word Hunt

▶ Fill in the missing word in each sentence.

1. Brin and Sang _____ in class.
 a. were
 b. we
 c. was

2. We can camp in a tent _____ in a cabin.
 a. on
 b. or
 c. one

3. Did Max _____ the laptop?
 a. you
 b. your
 c. use

4. If Tim runs _____, he will win.
 a. ahead
 b. are
 c. and

5. Grandmom _____ to visit us.
 a. call
 b. came
 c. can

6. Tess will _____ Lin a gift.
 a. give
 b. go
 c. good

7. Can you _____ on a trip with us?
 a. call
 b. come
 c. can

8. Liz _____ to swim in the pond.
 a. goes
 b. go
 c. good

9. Dad will _____ snacks for the picnic.
 a. my
 b. make
 c. me

10. We must get on the bus _____.
 a. no
 b. not
 c. now

*Use with **Teaching Guide**, page 524.*

Series 6 Review   Name

Series 6 Review	
6.1	fac<u>t</u>, draf<u>t</u>, hel<u>p</u>, sta<u>mp</u>
6.2	bli<u>nk</u>, wi<u>ng</u>
6.3	blan/ket, hab/it
6.4	san<u>d</u>, ten<u>t</u>
6.5	sight words

Word List

▶ Read the words from left to right. The words are new, but you have the skills to read them. Circle the words with **two syllables.**

> **bend   brings   bucket   bump   drifts   hands   panic   public   string   truck**

All Mixed Up

▶ **A.** Read each clue. Then, unscramble the words and write them on the lines.

1. The opposite of takes is _____. **grinbs**

2. Add ten plus ten. Do it ten times and you get this. _____ **rdudhne**

3. If something is true, it is this. _____ **cfta**

4. When you lend a hand, you do this. _____ **lpeh**

5. The opposite of *sit* is _____. **tdnas**

▶ **B.** Use words from the word bank to complete each sentence.

> **hint   tent   or   public   trunk**

6. What gift do you have for me? Can you give me a _____?

7. We can camp in this _____.

8. Do you like to sing _____ bang on the drums?

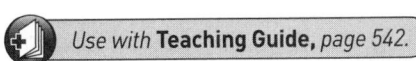 *Use with* **Teaching Guide,** *page 542.*

Name _____

Word List

▶ Read the words from left to right. Then, circle the words that begin with *sh* as in <u>sh</u>op.

> shack shell stack crash craft sell dish track
>
> shed fresh slang shift trash blend wish fits
>
> fish hundred

Rhyme It

Fill in each blank with a rhyming word from the word bank.

> shack   shop   shed   shell   ship

1. We like to _____ until we **drop**.

2. I spot a _____ at the bottom of the **well**.

3. Sam went on a **trip** on a big, tall _____.

4. I will live in a _____ with a cliff at my **back**!

5. A pig can make its **bed** in a barn or a _____.

Replace It

▶ Replace the underlined letter or letters in each word with *sh*. Write the new word on the line. The first one is done for you.

6. fre<u>t</u>   *fresh*

7. wi<u>n</u>   _____

8. trac<u>k</u>   _____

9. ru<u>ng</u>   _____

10. cra<u>mp</u>   _____

*Use with **Teaching Guide,** page 228.*

Name _____

Word List

▶ Read the words from left to right. Then, circle the words that begin with *ch* as in <u>*chop*</u>.

> champ cramp crash chat chill skill chop chunk
>
> planet chip bench limit inch skunk lunch rich
>
> stamp fresh

Review

<u>chop</u>

<u>inch</u>

A **digraph** is two letters that stand for one sound. The digraph *ch* stands for the sound you hear at the beginning of the word *chop* and at the end of the word *inch*.

Puzzle Fun

▶ Use words from the word bank to fill in the puzzle.

> champ   chat   chill   chop   chunk
> chip   bench   inch   lunch   rich

Across

1. to cut

3. If you win, you are this.

5. a small bit

6. How big is that bug? It is just an ___.

7. You eat this.

8. a big bit

Down

1. talk with a pal

2. If you get lots of cash, you are this.

3. to make cold

4. You can sit on this.

Name _____

Word List

▶ Read the words from left to right. Then, circle the words that begin with *ch* as in <u>*chop*</u>. Underline the words that end with -*tch* as in *ca<u>tch</u>*.

> check   bench   shift   chess   pinch   speck   branch   less
>
> pitch   rapid   chest   sketch   pits   catch   strand   chimp
>
> chick   stick

Complete It

▶ Complete each word by filling in the blank with *ch* or -*tch*. You may use a dictionary to help you. The first one is done for you.

1. bran *ch*

2. pi _____

3. pin _____

4. ske _____

5. lun _____

Replace It

▶ Replace the underlined letter or letters in each word with *ch* or -*tch*. Write the new word on the line. Check a dictionary if you are not sure which spelling to use.

6. ma<u>sh</u> _____

7. <u>s</u>lip _____

8. <u>f</u>lat _____

9. <u>i</u>nk _____

10. <u>m</u>ess _____

Spelling Pattern

sh as in *shop*, *ch* as in *chop*, *-tch* as in *catch*

Name

Word List

▶ Read the words from left to right. Then, circle the words that begin or end with *sh*. Underline the word that begins with *ch*. Put a star by the words that end with *-tch*.

camp fetch ship shock struck flag strand
fantastic chin blend shin draft brush cash
stretch scrap scratch flash

Sort It

▶ **A.** Find the words you marked in the word bank. Then, write them in the correct columns of the chart.

1. ch	2. -tch	3. sh

▶ **B.** Choose three words from above. Use each one in a sentence.

4. _____

5. _____

6. _____

Review

shop

chop

catch

- The digraph *sh* stands for the sound you hear at the beginning of the word *shop*.
- The digraph *ch* stands for the sound you hear at the beginning of the word *chop*.
- The letters *-tch* stand for the sound you hear at the end of the word *catch*.

 Use with **Teaching Guide,** *pages 228, 232.*

-es as in *benches*, *catches*

Name _____

Word List

▶ Read the words from left to right. Then, circle the words that have ending *-es*.

> **wishes**   **maps**   **brushes**   **jacket**   **sketch**   **bats**   **inches**
> **sketches**   **insist**   **branch**   **boxes**   **branches**   **pitches**
> **rushes**   **seven**   **stitches**   **taps**   **benches**

Add It On! Add It Up!

▶ Add the correct ending, *-s* or *-es*, to each word.
Write the new word on the line. Then, write how many syllables the word has. The first one is done for you.

		Ending	Word	Syllables
1.	buzz	*es*	*buzzes*	*2*
2.	ticket	_____	_____	_____
3.	mix	_____	_____	_____
4.	shift	_____	_____	_____
5.	ranch	_____	_____	_____
6.	king	_____	_____	_____
7.	wish	_____	_____	_____
8.	box	_____	_____	_____
9.	class	_____	_____	_____
10.	pitch	_____	_____	_____

Review

benches

catches

- Add ending *-es* to a noun that ends in *ch*, *sh*, *ss*, *x*, or *z* to make it plural.
- Add ending *-es* to a verb that ends in *ch*, *sh*, *ss*, *x*, or *z* to show action that takes place in the present.
- The ending *-es* adds a syllable to a word.

Use with **Teaching Guide,** *page 242.*

Name _____

Word List

▶ Read the words from left to right. Then, circle the words that you think are most difficult to spell.

> new   keep   were   use   could   now   where   goes   here
> grow   there   because   already   find   those   caught
> friend   who

Sentence Solver

▶ Use words from the word bank to complete each sentence.

where	because	could	caught	new
keep	find	those	grow	here

1. I lost my pen. Can you help me _____ it?

2. Mom said I _____ visit my friend Mitch.

3. Jon will _____ his CDs in a box.

4. I like this dog, but Liz likes _____ kittens.

5. Did you ask Jim _____ he is?

Clued In

▶ Find words from the word bank that match these definitions.

6. the reason why _____

7. to get bigger is to _____

8. not old _____

9. not there, but _____

10. in a trap _____

 *Use with **Teaching Guide,** page 524.*

Name _____

Word List

▶ Read the words from left to right. The words are new, but you have the skills to read them. Circle the words with ending **-es.**

| bunch chopsticks mash misses passes scratches |
| shops smashes stitch such |

Series 7 Review

7.1	shop, dish
7.2	chop, inch
7.3	chop, branch, catch
7.4	shop, chop, catch
7.5	benches, catches
7.6	sight words

Riddle Fun

▶ Use words from the word bank to answer the riddles.

| boxes | scratch | champ | grow | stretch |
| shop | find | fish | | |

1. When a cat is mad, it can do this. _____

2. I sell this and that. _____

3. Before you run, do this. _____

4. You can fill these up with your things. _____

5. I can swim in a pond. _____

6. If you win, you are this. _____

7. A plant gets big when it does this. _____

8. You do this to get back a thing that is lost. _____

9. Which words from the riddles above are used as naming words, or nouns?
   _____ _____ _____ _____

10. Which words from the riddles above are used as action words, or verbs?
    _____ _____ _____

*Use with **Teaching Guide,** page 542.*

Spelling Pattern

th as in <u>th</u>ank, <u>th</u>em

Name _____

Word List

▶ Read the words from left to right. Then, circle the words that begin with *th* as in *thank*.

ring	thing	fifth	flash	thin	cloth	thank	sketches
tent	path	fetch	tenth	than	pats	bath	them
ship	brush						

Review

thank

them

The **digraph** *th* stands for the sounds you hear at the beginning of the words *thank* and *them*.

Word Search

▶ Circle the words. The words can be down, across, or diagonal.

bath	thing	cloth	than
path	thank	tenth	them

```
p  b  y  t  l  t  c  q  t  p  w  h  z  z  s
w  a  e  h  u  q  h  n  j  l  a  t  m  k  n
j  t  m  i  v  i  w  a  b  h  m  q  i  i  t
r  h  b  n  q  n  l  t  n  z  k  e  v  w  o
g  g  u  g  r  f  h  m  x  c  l  o  t  h  v
f  s  z  m  b  q  e  q  t  m  t  z  x  n  b
s  i  u  n  h  r  k  z  w  z  e  h  i  g  u
t  h  a  n  k  j  m  n  q  y  l  h  e  o  u
q  u  u  i  g  j  a  f  p  a  t  h  f  m  y
l  l  u  q  f  t  e  n  t  h  j  p  q  h  q
```

Use with **Teaching Guide**, *page 236.*

Name _____

Word List

▶ Read the words from left to right. Then, circle the words that have a **digraph**.

> boxes   thick   jump   thump   craft   blush   match   plastic
> crunch   shrug   thrill   skill   jacket   math   scrub   then
> think   blink

Puzzle Fun

▶ Use words from the word bank to fill in the puzzle. Five across is done for you.

thick	blush	think	crunch	math
sixth	lash	thrill	match	shrug

Across

2.

3. a contest

5. This could show that you do not care.

8. When Tom runs fast, it gives him a _____.

9. after fifth

Down

1. I add it up in this class.

4. Beth likes snacks that make a ____.

6. What do you ____ of this CD?

7. I get red, or ____, if I trip.

8. not thin

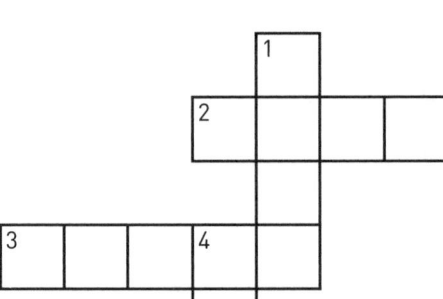

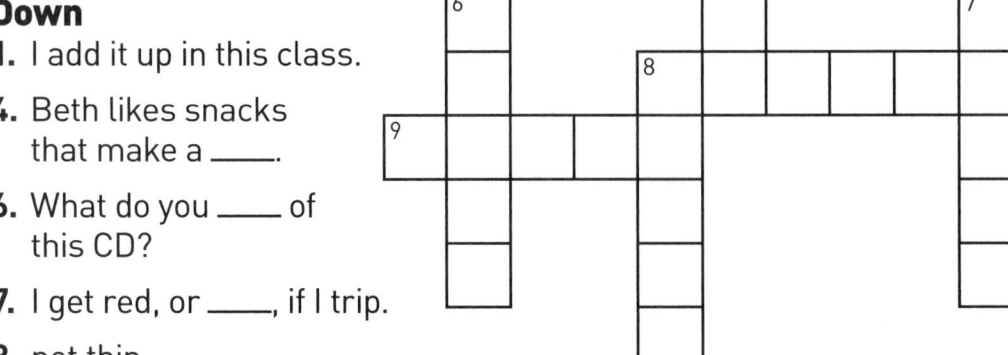

Use with **Teaching Guide,** *pages 228, 232, 236.*

-ing as in jumping

Name _____

Word List

▶ Read the words from left to right. Then, circle the words that have ending **-ing** as in **jumping**.

asking	sketching	stitches	rushes	catches	checking
pitches	catching	jumping	ticket	drastic	stretching
resting	sketches	spilling	fixing	cabinet	missing

Add It

▶ **A.** Add **-ing** and **-s** to each verb below. Underline the base word and circle the ending. The first one is done for you.

1. check _checking_ _checks_

5. risk _____ _____

2. rest _____ _____

6. act _____ _____

3. spill _____ _____

7. jump _____ _____

4. snack _____ _____

8. pick _____ _____

▶ **B.** Choose one word from above. Write two sentences. Use one form of the word in each sentence.

9. _____

10. _____

Review

He was jumping.
She is fixing the cab.
You will be stretching.

- An **ending** can be added to a **base word** to make other words.
- The ending **-ing** is added to verbs in some sentences to tell about things that happen in the present, past, and future.
- The ending **-ing** adds a syllable to a word.

Use with **Teaching Guide**, page 246.

-ed as in planted

Name _____

Word List

▶ Read the words from left to right. Then, circle the words that have ending **-ed** as in **planted**.

> lifted drifted crunch rested lashes landed rushing
>
> resting ended lasted acted plants thrill listed
>
> listing blushes blended trusted

TM & © Scholastic Inc. All rights reserved.

Review
planted
ended
rested
• The ending **-ed** can be added to verbs to tell about things that happened in the past.
• The ending **-ed** can add a syllable to a word.

Add It

▶ Add **-ed** to each verb. The first one is done for you.

1. hint *hinted*
2. rest _____
3. blend _____
4. plant _____
5. end _____

6. test _____
7. act _____
8. lift _____
9. drift _____
10. list _____

▶ Sentence Solver

Choose words you wrote above to finish each sentence. One is done for you.

11. Jen *hinted* that she would like a new jacket.

12. The film _____ at ten.

13. Meg _____ upset when she lost her ring.

14. Lin _____ the crops.

15. I went back to bed and _____.

16. The raft _____ in the pond.

Use with **Teaching Guide**, page 246.

-ed as in jumped, spilled

Name

Word List

▶ Read the words from left to right. Then, circle the words with ending **-ed**.

mixed	jumped	branches	blocked	catching	risking
jumping	passed	filled	asking	bumped	missed
resting	rushed	inches	spilling	spilled	tricked

Review

jum<u>ped</u>

spill<u>ed</u>

- In some words, the **-ed** ending is pronounced as the sound letter *t* stands for.
- In other words, the **-ed** ending is pronounced as the sound letter *d* stands for.

Sentence Solver

▶ **A.** Use words from the word bank to complete each sentence.

blocked	dressed	spilled	rushed	yelled
mixed	jumped	passed	packed	missed

1. I _____ the bus, so I had to run to class.

2. Mom _____ her bag for the trip.

3. My dog _____ up to get a snack.

4. Zack _____ to get here. He didn't want to miss the fun!

5. I _____ my milk and had to mop it up.

6. Juan _____ the dish to Dad at lunch.

7. Trish got _____ and put on her jacket.

8. A rock _____ the path, so the truck had to go back.

▶ **B.** Find the words you did not use. Use each one in a sentence.

9. _____

10. _____

 Use with **Teaching Guide,** *page 246.*

**-ing as in visiting,
-ed as in visited**

Name

Review

visiting

visited

The endings *-ing* and *-ed* are added to verbs to tell when something happens.

Word List

▶ Read the words from left to right. Then, circle the words with ending *-ing*. Underline the words with ending *-ed*.

expected   catches   invested   benches   visiting

pitches   insisted   hundred   wishes   expecting

limited   dismissing   expanding   invented   stitches

ticket   visited   limiting

Add It

▶ Add *-ed* or *-ing* to the word in bold type to complete each sentence. The first one is started for you.

1. visit

We ___*visited*___ Jess last week.

Sang is _____ his friend Liz now.

2. finish

Soon, I will be _____ this task.

Max already _____ his sketch.

3. expect

Dad _____ to get on the bus, but it did not come.

Tran is _____ to see the film at six.

4. insist

Ms. Penn is _____ that we do well on the test!

Mom _____ that the dog not jump on the desk.

5. invent

Jon _____ a new cup. It will not tip!

Brin is _____ ink that you can not see!

Use with **Teaching Guide,** *page 246.*

Sight Words

Name _____

Word List

▶ Read the words from left to right. Then, circle the words you think are most difficult to spell.

all	because	under	ahead	caught	our	say	their
came	almost	where	give	away	want	use	when
something	were						

Sentence Solver

▶ **A.** Use words from the word bank to complete each sentence.

when	all	want	almost	under
away	their	our	something	say

1. I _____ a kitten.

2. Will Dad _____ *yes* or *no* if we ask him for a pet?

3. There is _____ in this box for you.

4. Look _____ the desk for your pen.

5. _____ can we have a picnic?

▶ **B.** Use each remaining word from the word bank in a sentence.

6. _____

7. _____

8. _____

9. _____

10. _____

 *Use with **Teaching Guide**, page 524.*

Word List

▶ Read the words from left to right. The words are new, but you have the skills to read them. Circle the words with **two syllables**.

blinked paths handed listing punishing testing
thanked acting thinking within

Series 8 Review	
8.1	thank, them
8.2	lash, match, crunch
8.3	jumping, fixing
8.4	planted, ended
8.5	jumped, spilled
8.6	visiting, visited
8.7	sight words

Riddle Fun

▶ **A.** Fill in each blank with a word part or spelling pattern from the box below.

-ed   -ing   th   sh

1. I wi __ __ I had something to snack on.
    1

2. I __ __ ink math is fun.
    2

3. Lin is jump __ __ __ up and down.
    3

4. Max likes visit __ __ __ his pals.
    4

5. Jen miss __ __ the bus.
    5 6

▶ **B.** Match the letters above to the numbered lines below. It will give you the answer to this riddle.

What did one chip say to the other?

6. __ __ all w __ __ o for a __ __ p?
   1 2   5 4   6 3

Name

Word List

▶ Read the words from left to right. Then, circle any three words that have an unstressed syllable with the **schwa vowel sound**.

> expected   distant   metal   match   habit   listed   passed
>
> pants   petal   infant   instant   level   resting   problem
>
> atlas   pedal   hushed   chicken

Review

infant

problem

The vowel sound in a **closed syllable** is usually short. But when a syllable is unstressed, its vowel sound may get "clipped," or reduced to schwa.

Split It

▶ **A.** Draw a line to split each word into syllables. Underline the stressed syllable. The first one is done for you.

1. med|al   **3.** instant   **5.** talent

2. pedals   **4.** children

▶ **B.** Draw a line to split each word into syllables. Circle the letter that stands for the **schwa sound** in the unstressed syllable. The first one is done for you.

6. at|l(a)s   **8.** infant   **10.** problem

7. distant   **9.** constant

Write It

▶ Choose four words from Split It. Use each one in a sentence.

11. _____

12. _____

13. _____

14. _____

Use with **Teaching Guide,** page 254.

Unstressed Closed Syllables (*i, o, u*)

Name _____

Word List

▶ Read the words from left to right. Then, circle any three words that have an unstressed syllable with the **schwa vowel sound**.

bottom	talent	checking	trusted	gallon	recommend	
collecting	tonsil	brushes	custom	random	medal	
camps	lemon	catches	level	common	melon	

Review

tonsil

custom

cactus

The vowel sound in a **closed syllable** is usually short. But when a syllable is unstressed, its vowel sound may get "clipped," or reduced to schwa.

Split It

▶ **A.** Draw a line to split each word into syllables. Underline the stressed syllable. Circle the vowel that stands for the **schwa sound** in the unstressed syllable. The first one is done for you.

1. bot|tom
2. blossom
3. campus
4. gallon
5. buttons

6. random
7. cotton
8. lesson
9. canyon
10. common

11. tonsil
12. melon
13. lemon
14. cactus
15. recommend

▶ **B.** Read each question about the words in Split It. Write your answer on the blank.

16. Which word has the most syllables? _____

17. How many syllables does it have? _____

18. Which words have the schwa sound spelled with the letter **u**?

   _____   _____

19. Which word has the schwa sound spelled with the letter **i**?

   _____

Use with **Teaching Guide,** *page 254.*

Consonant + -le

Name

Word List

▶ Read the words from left to right. Then, circle the words with **consonant + -le** as in *angle*.

> ankle   pedals   tremble   bottle   riddle   mumble
>
> simple   buttons   melon   sample   candid   publishing
>
> camel   crumble   tricked   middle   puddle

Review

angle

giggle

The **consonant + -le** pattern usually forms its own syllable. You can split a word with the consonant + -le pattern before the consonant to help make it easier to read.

Split It

▶ Draw a line to split each word into syllables. The first one is done for you.

1. an|gle
2. single
3. handle

4. tremble
5. middle
6. puddle

7. riddle
8. giggle
9. simple

Complete It

▶ Complete each word by filling in the blank with the correct syllable from the box. You may use a dictionary to help you.

> ble   dle   gle   kle   ple   tle

10. sim_____

11. rid_____

12. mum_____

13. gig_____

14. bot_____

15. can_____

*Use with **Teaching Guide**, page 258.*

Consonant + -al, -el

Name _____

Word List

► Read the words from left to right. Then, underline the words with the **consonant + -al** pattern and circle the words with the **consonant + -el** pattern.

flannel	visiting	signal	renting	funnel	tunnel
rental	mammal	dented	pitches	metal	tonsil
channel	dental	kennel	gallon	sandal	distant

Circle It

► Circle the word in each row that has the **consonant + -al** or **consonant + -el** pattern.

1. rental	button	laptop
2. muffin	cabin	sandal
3. insist	funnel	contest
4. flannel	napkin	rabbit
5. hundred	mammal	basket

Build It

► Build words using one word part from each box. Then, write the words on the lines below. The first one is done for you.

Beginning				
chan	den	mam	sig	san

End				
dal	mal	tal	nel	nal

6. _____ *channel* _____

7. _____

8. _____

9. _____

10. _____

Sight Words | Name _____

Word List

▶ Read the words from left to right. Then, circle the words you think you have used today.

says	when	under	down	saw	away	kind	more
something	because	over	almost	does	show		
these	want	made	where				

Sentence Solver

▶ Use words from the word bank to complete each sentence.

says	does	down	kind	made
more	over	saw	show	these

1. Kent helps pets that live in the kennel. He is very _____ .

2. The kids are jumping up and _____, splashing in the puddle.

3. Dad got a mix and _____ muffins for us.

4. Do you want _____ or less?

5. Mom _____, "Finish your job, and then you can swim."

6. What _____ Franklin like to do for fun?

7. I like _____ stamps, not those.

8. Min _____ a dog that acted in a film!

9. Will you _____ me your new TV?

10. The milk spilled _____ the top of the cup.

 Use with **Teaching Guide,** *page 524.*

Name

Series 9 Review

9.1	infant, problem
9.2	ton̄sil, cus̲tom, cactus̲
9.3	an̲gle, gig̲gle
9.4	den̲tal, tun̲nel
9.5	sight words

Word List

▶ Read the words from left to right. The words are new, but you have the skills to read them. Circle any two words with **unstressed closed syllables.**

> travels   buckle   cotton   fossils   ribbon   talented
>
> happen   lessons   puzzles   settle

Split It

▶ Draw a line to split each word into syllables. Underline the stressed syllable. Then, circle the vowel sound in the unstressed syllable. The first one is done for you.

1. les|s(o)n
2. ribbon

3. infant
4. cactus

5. fossil
6. happen

Complete It

▶ Complete each word by filling in the blank with the correct syllable from the box. You may use a dictionary to help you.

> dle   fle   gle   tle   tal   nel

7. sin_____

8. ket_____

9. can_____

10. fun_____

11. den_____

12. shuf_____

Just for Fun

▶ Say this tongue twister five times fast!

Simple shuffle.

 *Use with **Teaching Guide,** page 542.*

Name _____

Make New Words

▶ Add *e* to each word and write the new word. Then, write a sentence using the new word. The first one is done for you.

1.	hat	_hate_	*I hate missing the bus.*
2.	cap	_____	_____
3.	can	_____	_____
4.	tap	_____	_____
5.	rat	_____	_____

Review

c<u>a</u>p<u>e</u>

g<u>a</u>me

- These words have the **long *a* vowel sound**. The long *a* sound is the same as the letter's name in the alphabet.

- The **long *a* sound** can be spelled in many ways. Letter *a* stands for the long *a* sound in words with a vowel-consonant-*e* pattern (**VCe**).

Circle It

▶ First, circle the words with the long *a* sound as in *mate*.
Then, underline the words with the short *a* sound as in *mat*.
The first one is done for you.

6. (wave)   (gate)   <u>cat</u>   <u>man</u>   <u>ran</u>   (maze)

7. tan   cane   tap   ban   game   map

8. rake   sat   pan   cape   nap   fame

9. sale   cake   hat   same   bat   sap

10. wake   man   cab   pat   ram   tape

11. tab   late   name   ham   bake   van

12. take   tag   pad   fade   jam   date

Use with **Teaching Guide,** *page 262.*

Name

Rhyme It

▶ Read each poem. Fill in the blanks with a rhyming word from the word bank.

dime	dive	nine	hive	bike

1. Lin is just **five,**
   But she can swim and _____ .

2. Which do you **like,**
   The truck or the _____?

3. Can you get a **lime,**
   For just a _____?

4. To make a call on the **line,**
   Just press number _____.

5. The bees are **live.**
   Stand back from their _____!

Link It

▶ Finish each word chain. Change one letter at a time. Some are done for you.

6. Go from **cane** to **bike**.
cane
cake
bake
bike

7. Go from **cake** to **time**.
cake
tame

8. Go from **sale** to **mile**.
sale
tile

 *Use with **Teaching Guide**, page 266.*

Name _____

Review

cape

kite

These words have the **vowel-consonant-e** pattern **(VCe)**. This pattern signals that the vowel sound is long.

Fix It

▶ One word in each sentence is missing final **e**. Find the word and cross it out. Then, write the word correctly. The first one is **done for you**.

1. Use ~~twin~~ to make a strap. _____*twine*_____

2. Kate takes a trip on a plan. _____

3. Your spin is made of bones. _____

4. The sun will shin. _____

5. Do not scrap your leg. _____

6. My pants have a red strip. _____

7. Kayla got a good grad on her quiz. _____

Does It Rhyme?

▶ Read each word pair below. Write **Yes** if the words rhyme. Write **No** if they do not rhyme. Then, write a new rhyming word for the word that is underlined. The first one is **done for you**.

	Word Pair		Rhyme?	New Rhyme
8.	strike	<u>grade</u>	*no*	*trade*
9.	spine	<u>twine</u>	_____	_____
10.	prize	<u>flake</u>	_____	_____
11.	<u>strive</u>	drive	_____	_____
12.	<u>smile</u>	shade	_____	_____

 *Use with **Teaching Guide**, pages 262, 266.*

Soft *c* as in *cell*

Name

Review

c̲ell

dan̲ce

When consonant *c* is followed by letters *e, i,* or *y,* it stands for the sound you hear in c̲ell and dan̲ce.

Circle It

▶ Read each word. Circle all the words in which ***c*** stands for the sound you hear at the beginning of ***cell***.

1. cent   cab   mice
2. cat   dance   can
3. cape   space   fence
4. cell   cane   face

Sort It

▶ Read the words in the word bank. Then, write each one in the correct column of the chart.

| prince | face | camp | twice | cake |
| cuff | chance | cut | cent | fence |

5. *c* as in *cell*	6. *c* as in *cat*

*Use with **Teaching Guide**, page 270.*

Name

Circle It

▶ Read each word. Circle all the words in which **g** stands for the sound you hear at the beginning of **gem**.

1. cage	edge	game
2. age	gap	page
3. judge	stage	gas
4. gate	bridge	range

Review

gem

bridge

• When consonant **g** is followed by letters **e**, **i**, or **y**, it can stand for the sound you hear in **gem** and **page**.

• The letters **dge** stand for the sound you hear at the end of **bridge**.

Sentence Solver

▶ Use words from the word bank to complete each sentence.

bridge	edge	gem	judge
page	change	age	stage

5. Lane wants to act on a _____ .

6. She has a big _____ in her ring.

7. Nick has to _____ the tire on the van.

8. We will cross the _____ to get to the other side.

9. What is the _____ of your dog? Is he five or six?

10. Dad will be the _____ of the spelling contest.

11. Do not stand too close to the _____ of that pit.

12. I will use tape to fix the rip on this _____ .

Word Parts

Suffixes
-ment, -ness

Name

Build It

▶ Build new words by adding suffixes to the base words. Write each word on the line.

1. content + ment = _____

2. ill + ness = _____

3. punish + ment = _____

4. thick + ness = _____

5. quick + ness = _____

> ### Review
>
> content**ment**
>
> **sad**ness
>
> - A **suffix** is a word part added at the end of a base word to change its meaning.
> - The suffix *-ment* changes the base word *content* from an adjective to a noun.
> - The suffix *-ness* changes the base word *sad* from an adjective to a noun.

Add It

▶ Add *-ment* or *-ness* to each underlined word. Then, write the new word on the line. One is done for you.

6. This <u>sick</u> ___*ness*___ makes my dog nap all the time.___*sickness*___

7. We missed the film because of Dan's <u>late</u> _____ . _____

8. You can see the <u>content</u> _____ on Mom's face when she is glad.

   _____

9. There are ten boxes in this <u>ship</u> _____ . _____

10. I like the <u>still</u> _____ of the camp when the sun has just

    come up. _____

Sight Words   Name

Puzzle Fun

▶ Use words from the word bank to fill in the puzzle.

about	always	between	how	many
never	together	too	why	yesterday

Across

3. What is that film _____?

7. I went on a long bike ride _____ .

9. Can you tell me _____ to make muffins?

10. I _____ go camping because I do not have a tent.

Down

1. There are so _____ gifts! How can I pick just one?

2. Chad and Blake sit _____ on the bus.

4. I am going to the lake. Do you want to come, _____?

5. Can you tell me _____ Dave has a big smile on his face?

6. I sit _____ Max and Katelin.

8. Jasmin _____ wins races because she is very quick.

 Use with **Teaching Guide,** page 524.

Word List

▶ Read the words from left to right. The words are new, but you have the skills to read them. Circle any three words with a **long vowel sound**.

brave	gentleness	hinge	life	investment	name
place	rides	slides	take		

Series 10 Review

10.1	cape, game
10.2	kite, bike
10.3	cape, kite
10.4	cell, dance
10.5	gem, bridge
10.6	contentment, sadness
10.7	sight words

Complete It

▶ Complete each word by filling in the blanks with *a*, *e*, or *i*. The first one is done for you.

1. A nice plum.   r _i_ p _e_

2. This is fun to ride.   b ___ k ___

3. It will fix a rip.   t ___ p ___

4. 4 + 1   f ___ v ___

Sort It

▶ Read each word in the word bank. Then, write it in the correct column of the chart below.

place	gentle	candle	game	cape
gap	nice	gym		

5. *c* as in *spice*	6. *c* as in *cast*	7. *g* as in *gem*	8. *g* as in *gas*

*Use with **Teaching Guide**, page 542.*

Spelling Pattern

Long *o* as in *hope*

Name

Review

h<u>o</u>p<u>e</u>

n<u>o</u>t<u>e</u>

- These words have the **long *o* vowel sound**. The long *o* sound is the same as the letter's name in the alphabet.
- The **long *o* sound** can be spelled in many ways. Letter *o* stands for the long *o* sound in words with a vowel-consonant-*e* pattern (**VC*e***).

Circle It

▶ Read the words. Then, circle the words in each row with the **long *o* sound** you hear in *hope*.

1. broke	hot	dome	box	dot	hole
2. pod	quote	rode	mop	nose	shock
3. joke	lock	shop	note	cone	dog
4. hop	hope	globe	nod	shone	dock
5. stove	sock	stomp	stone	top	froze

Word Search

▶ Circle the words. The words can be down, across, or diagonal.

broke	**cone**	**dome**	**globe**	**hole**
hope	**joke**	**nose**	**note**	**quote**

k	u	a	c	z	b	h	j	u	q
h	g	l	o	b	e	r	x	v	r
j	o	k	e	t	z	c	o	n	e
m	z	l	c	q	o	c	t	k	e
b	d	d	e	w	f	l	m	u	e
j	h	o	d	v	r	d	f	q	z
s	o	c	m	v	q	u	o	t	e
l	p	m	o	e	z	l	w	x	y
g	e	q	n	o	s	e	r	z	e
o	d	f	q	g	z	n	o	t	e

Use with **Teaching Guide**, *page 276.*

Long *u* as in *cube*

Name _____

Circle It

▶ **A.** Read the words. Then, circle the words in each row with the **long *u* sound** you hear in *fuse*.

1. muse	hug	huge	bike
2. lake	cute	fume	cut
3. cube	cub	nice	mule
4. late	fuse	mute	fuss

▶ **B.** Write the words you circled in Part A. Circle the letters that stand for the **long *u* sound**.

5. _____   **9.** _____

6. _____   **10.** _____

7. _____   **11.** _____

8. _____

Review

cube

fuse

• These words have the **long *u* vowel sound**. The long *u* sound is the same as the letter's name in the alphabet.

• The **long *u* sound** can be spelled in several ways. Letter *u* can stand for the long *u* sound in words with a vowel-consonant-*e* pattern (VC*e*).

Link It

▶ Finish each word chain. You may change a letter or add a letter. Some are done for you.

12. Go from **hat** to **cute**.
hat
hut
cut
cute

13. Go from **tab** to **cube**.
_____
_____
_____
cube

14. Go from **take** to **fume**.
_____
tame
_____
fume

Use with **Teaching Guide,** page 280.

Syllable Types

VCe Syllables

Name

Split It

▶ Draw a line to split each word into syllables. Underline the syllable that has a long vowel sound.
Hint: One word has three syllables.

1. compose
2. mistake
3. basement

4. tribute
5. invite
6. advice

7. online
8. compute
9. distribute

> ### Review
>
> online
>
> invite
>
> Syllables with the vowel-consonant-*e* pattern (**VCe**) have a long vowel sound. When you split a word with this pattern into syllables, keep the letters of the VCe pattern together.

Sort It

▶ Read the words in the word bank. Then, write each one in the correct column of the chart.

distribute	globe	compute	tribute
cube	compose	advice	fuse
admires	contribute	basement	online

10. 1-syllable words	11. 2-syllable words	12. 3-syllable words

*Use with **Teaching Guide**, page 284.*

More VCe Syllables

Name _____

Split It

▶ Draw a line to split each word into syllables. Underline the syllable with the **vowel-consonant-e** pattern in each word. The first one is done for you.

1. col|lide
2. explode
3. lemonade

4. dispute
5. illustrate
6. nickname

7. enclose
8. inflate
9. translate

Review

inside

translate

Syllables with the vowel-consonant-e pattern (**VCe**) have a long vowel sound. When you split a word with this pattern into syllables, keep the letters of the VCe pattern together.

All Mixed Up

▶ Unscramble each of the words and use them to complete the sentences.

nickname	translate	engrave	suppose
explode	lemonade	inflate	

10. Cristal sells _____ that she makes with fresh lemons. **onlemdae**

11. I _____ I can help you fix your van. **ssuppoe**

12. Can you _____ this? It is in Spanish. **lsertnata**

13. I need to _____ the tires on my bike or they will be flat. **niftlae**

14. Dad will _____ Mom's name on a bracelet. **genreva**

15. My name is Tomas, but my _____ is Tom. **kcinmean**

16. The balloon will _____ if you pop it. **xpeldoe**

Use with **Teaching Guide,** *page 284.*

Prefixes
un-, non-, de-

Name _____

Circle It

▶ Circle the word in each row that has a **prefix**. Then, write the meaning of the word on the line. The first one is done for you.

> **un-** = "not" or "the opposite of"
>
> **non-** = "not" or "the opposite of"
>
> **de-** = "the opposite of"

1. nostril   (nonstop)   nose   _not stopping_

2. dented   dental   defrost   _____

3. unpacked   under   until   _____

Match It

▶ Combine a prefix from **Box A** with a word from **Box B** to make a word that matches each clue below. You may use a dictionary to help you. The first one is done for you.

Box A	un- non- de-

Box B	slip compose stop lock ripe

4. to rot   _decompose_

5. You can run on this and not skid.   _____

6. If something goes and goes, it is this.   _____

7. Use a key to open something.   _____

8. If a plum is not good to eat, it can be this.   _____

Use with **Teaching Guide**, *page 532.*

Sight Words

Name _____

Sentence Solver

▶ Use words from the word bank to complete each sentence.

along	below	put	different
heavy	every	off	should
thought	word		

1. Nate has on a _____ cap each time I see him.

2. Megan _____ the dishes in the sink.

3. Is that box _____, or can you lift it?

4. Switch _____ the lamp when you go to bed.

5. What _____ I bring for lunch?

6. I _____ the game was at six, but it was at five.

7. Will you bring your dog _____ when you go on a trip?

8. _____ time I am with Devin, we have a good time.

9. The attic is on top of the kitchen, and the basement is _____ it.

10. There are five letters in the _____ *quote.*

Write It

▶ Choose two words from the word bank. Use each one in a sentence.

11. _____

12. _____

 Use with **Teaching Guide,** *page 524.*

Word List

▶ Read the words from left to right. The words are new, but you have the skills to read them. Circle the words with a **prefix**.

decode	drove	entire	escapes	frustrate	home
inspire	nonprofit	reptile	unbend		

Series 11 Review

11.1	hope, note
11.2	cube, fuse
11.3	online, invite
11.4	inside, translate
11.5	unlock, nonfat, defrost,
11.6	sight words

Add It

▶ Complete each word by adding **un-, non-,** or **de-**. Then, write the new word on the line.

1. I _____ packed my bag when I got home. _____

2. We drove _____ stop to L.A. _____

3. Dad will _____ frost the chicken for lunch. _____

Build It

▶ Read each clue below. Then, choose the correct letters from the box to complete each word. You may use a dictionary to help you. The first one is done for you.

a	e	i	o	u

4. Where you live: h _o_ m _e_   **7.** Give out: distrib ___ t ___

5. A snake: rept ___ l ___   **8.** Go on the Web: onl ___ n ___

6. Get away: esc ___ p ___

*Use with **Teaching Guide,** page 542.*

Word Parts

Ending *-ing* (drop *e*)

Name _____

Add It

▶ Read each word. Then add *-ing* to the base word and write it on the line. Write a sentence with the new word. The first one is done for you.

Base Word + *-ing*	**Sentence**
1. giggle _giggling_	_Grace is giggling at my jokes._
2. slide _____	_____
3. escape _____	_____
4. vote _____	_____

> **Review**
>
> chasing
>
> skating
>
> • When *-ing* is added to a base word that ends in *e*, the *e* is dropped.
> • The *-ing* ending can be used with verbs to tell about actions in the present, past, or future.

Choose It

▶ Choose the correct form of each word and write it on the line.

5. Are you _____ for Shannon for class president?

   vote, voting

6. Sam and Alex _____ me with my twin sister.

   confuse, confusing

7. Did you _____ Kristin?

   invite, inviting

8. Who is _____ the problem?

   handle, handling

9. I like to _____ at the rink.

   skate, skating

10. The plane is _____ in the sky.

    glide, gliding

 *Use with* **Teaching Guide,** *page 290.*

Ending -*ing* (with doubling)

Name

Add It

▶ **A.** Read each word. Add ending -*ing* to the base word. Double the final consonant when needed. One is done for you.

Base Word	+ -*ing*
1. admit	admit(t)ing
2. chat	
3. bat	
4. step	
5. jump	
6. scrub	
7. chop	
8. skim	
9. lift	

Review

chatting

winning

When -*ing* is added to a base word that ends with a single consonant after a vowel, the final consonant is doubled.

▶ **B.** Complete each sentence by adding -*ing* to the word in bold type.

10. Nicole loves to tell jokes. She is always _____ around. **kid**

11. Rob and I like to run. We go _____ by the lake. **jog**

12. Lim is _____ with Granddad online. **chat**

13. We are _____ the van so that we can stretch our legs. **stop**

14. Jon is _____ the dishes. **scrub**

Use with **Teaching Guide**, page 294.

Ending -ed (drop e)

Name

Fix It

▶ Fix the sentences below by adding ending **-ed** to the underlined words. Write the new words in the blanks. The first one is done for you.

Review

biked

joked

When **-ed** is added to a base word that ends in e, the e is dropped.

1. We <u>bike</u> five miles yesterday. _____biked_____

2. I <u>vote</u> for Matt to be the class president. _____

3. Max <u>dislike</u> the sandwich he had for lunch. _____

4. Mom <u>joke</u> that she is always the last one at the table. _____

5. Liz <u>travel</u> to six different states. _____

6. The cat <u>doze</u> by the fire. _____

7. She <u>ask</u> for a glass of lemonade. _____

8. Dan <u>smile</u> when he won the contest. _____

9. They <u>rest</u> and then got back in the game. _____

10. Franklin <u>wave</u> to me from the bus. _____

Write It

▶ Choose four words that you made in Fix It. Use each one in a sentence.

11. _____

12. _____

13. _____

14. _____

*Use with **Teaching Guide**, page 290.*

Ending -ed
(with doubling)

Name

Add It

► **A.** Add ending **-ed** to each word. Double the final consonant when needed. Write the new word on the line.

<table>
<tr><td>1.</td><td>brag _____</td><td>5.</td><td>stop _____</td></tr>
<tr><td>2.</td><td>hope _____</td><td>6.</td><td>mop _____</td></tr>
<tr><td>3.</td><td>trim _____</td><td>7.</td><td>wash _____</td></tr>
<tr><td>4.</td><td>admit_____</td><td>8.</td><td>joke _____</td></tr>
</table>

> **Review**
>
> blog**ged**
>
> grin**ned**
>
> When **-ed** is added to a base word that ends with a single consonant after a vowel, the final consonant is doubled.

► **B.** Complete each sentence by adding **-ed** to the word in bold type. The first one is done for you.

9. The dog _____*wagged*_____ its tail. **wag**

10. Donna _____ her next trip. **plan**

11. Jin _____ my new jacket **admire**

12. Greg _____ this film to me. **recommend**

13. We _____ online in our computer class. **blog**

14. James _____ at the game yesterday. **pitch**

15. We _____ for Brin when she sang in the contest. **clap**

16. I _____ my leg, but I am fine. **scrape**

17. Janet _____ when she saw the kitten. **grin**

18. Chad _____ the text before the quiz. **skim**

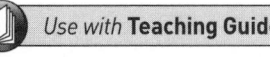 *Use with* **Teaching Guide,** *page 294.*

Sight Words | Name

Find It

▶ Use words from the word bank to find the opposites.

> took   above   answer

1. The opposite of *ask* is _____.

2. The opposite of *gave* is _____.

3. The opposite of *below* is _____.

Sentence Solver

▶ Use words from the word bank to complete each sentence.

> believe   both   nature   leave
> only   through   would

4. What time did you _____ the festival?

5. Can you _____ we won that match? It was a close game!

6. We hiked on the path that goes _____ the hills.

7. Plants and grass are part of _____.

8. You can have two snacks. Take _____ an apple and a plum.

9. There is _____ one grape left.

10. _____ you like to go swimming?

Use with **Teaching Guide,** *page 524.*

Name

Series 12 Review

12.1	chasing, skating
12.2	chatting, winning
12.3	biked, joked
12.4	blogged, grinned
12.5	sight words

Word List

▶ Read the words from left to right. The words are new, but you have the skills to read them. Circle the words that have doubled consonants before their endings.

admired   diving   driving   drumming   faded   hummed

rapping   running   snapping   trading

Define It

▶ Choose two words from the word bank. Find the meaning of the words in a dictionary. Write the definitions.

1. _____

2. _____

Finish It

▶ Complete each sentence by writing the **-ed** or **-ing** form of the word.

3. **sip**

Ashton is _____ his drink.

Max _____ his glass of milk.

4. **admire**

I have _____ that band for a long time.

Kim is _____ Jen's ring.

Add It

▶ Add **-ed** and **-ing** to each verb below.

5. fade   _____   _____

6. drum   _____   _____

 Use with **Teaching Guide,** page 542.

y as a Vowel as in *cr*y, *g*y*m, happ*y

Name

Sort It

▶ Each word in the word bank has the letter *y*. Read each word. Then, write it in the correct column of the chart below. One is done for you.

cry	gym	spy	symbol	happy
system	hungry	fly	safety	shy
myth	city			

1. long *e* spelled *y*	2. long *i* spelled *y*	3. short *i* spelled *y*
_____	*cry*	_____
_____	_____	_____
_____	_____	_____
_____	_____	_____

Review

cry

gym

happy

- When a word has one syllable and ends with letter *y*, the *y* can stand for the **long *i* sound** as in *cry*.

- Letter *y* can also stand for the **short *i* sound** when it is between two consonants as in *gym*.

- When a word has more than one syllable and ends with letter *y*, the *y* can stand for the **long *e* sound** as in *happy*.

Write It

▶ Choose four words from Sort It. Use each one in a sentence.

4. _____

5. _____

6. _____

7. _____

Use with **Teaching Guide,** *page 300.*

Word Parts

Suffixes -y, -ly

Name _____

Build It

▶ Make new words by adding the **suffixes** below to the words in bold type. Write each word on the line. You may use a dictionary to help you.

Suffixes	
-ly = "like" or "in a _____ way"	*-y* = "being, having, able to"

1. _____
having **luck**

2. _____
able to **trick**

3. _____
in a **brisk** way

4. _____
in a **rapid** way

5. _____
being a **risk**

6. _____
in a **safe** way

7. _____
having an **itch**

8. _____
having **spice**

9. _____
being a **mess**

Review

bris<u>kly</u>

trick<u>y</u>

• A **suffix** is a word part that is added to the end of a base word to change the word's meaning or part of speech.

• Suffixes *-ly* and *-y* can be added to the end of a base word.

• When *-y* is added to a base word that ends in *e*, the *e* is dropped.

Find It

▶ Use words from the word bank to answer the questions.

lucky	briskly	spicy	rapidly

10. Which word tells about someone who wins a lot?

_____

11. Which word can tell about a hot dish? _____

12. Which two words can tell about how fast someone runs?

_____ _____

Name

Add It

▶ Add **-ed** and **-es** to each word. The first one is done for you.

	-ed	-es
1. spy	*spied*	*spies*
2. multiply		
3. try		
4. wish		
5. classify		
6. dry		
7. hatch		
8. supply		

Fix It

▶ Fix these sentences by adding **-es**, **-ed**, or **-ly** to each underlined word. The first one is done for you.

9. We visited five **city** on our trip. _____ *cities* _____

10. The jet **fly** quickly. _____

11. Jeff grinned **happy** when he won the spelling contest.

_____

12. I **try** to run a mile in gym class. _____

13. We ate the grapes **hungry**. _____

14. I **multiply** 9 and 9 and got 81. _____

Use with **Teaching Guide,** *page 304.*

wh as in _whale_
ph as in _phone_

Name

Replace It

▶ Replace the underlined letter or letters in each word with **wh** or **ph**. Write the new word on the line. Check a dictionary if you are not sure which spelling to use. The first one is done for you.

1. <u>b</u>ite   _white_

2. <u>t</u>one   _____

3. <u>s</u>ale   _____

4. <u>t</u>rim   _____

5. <u>ch</u>ip   _____

6. <u>v</u>ase   _____

7. <u>b</u>risk   _____

8. gra<u>m</u>   _____

Review

<u>wh</u>ale

<u>ph</u>one

• A **digraph** is two letters that stand for one sound. The digraph **wh** stands for the sound you hear at the beginning of the word **whale**.

• The letters **ph** stand for the sound you hear at the beginning of the word **phone**.

Write It

▶ Choose four words you wrote in Replace It. Use each one in a sentence.

9. _____

10. _____

11. _____

12. _____

Use with **Teaching Guide,** _page 308._

Sight Words   Name

Puzzle Fun

▶ Use words from the word bank to fill in the puzzle.

any	been	even	great	please
know	laugh	move	other	really

Across

1. Kelly's jokes always make me _____.

5. Is there _____ a quiz, or was Ms. Lan kidding?

7. Here is one sock. Where is the _____?

8. Where has James _____? I did not see him at the game.

10. Do you _____ how to make a spicy snack mix?

Down

2. I had a _____ time at the concert. I danced a lot!

3. Are there _____ plums left? I would like one.

4. It is nice to say _____ and thank you.

6. Jenny has to _____ to a new city. I will miss her.

9. The bike path is not bumpy. It is nice and _____.

*Use with **Teaching Guide**, page 524.*

Series 13 Review | Name _____

Series 13 Review	
13.1	cr<u>y</u>, g<u>y</u>m, happ<u>y</u>
13.2	brisk<u>ly</u>, trick<u>y</u>
13.3	cit<u>ie</u>s, dr<u>ie</u>d, happ<u>i</u>ly
13.4	<u>wh</u>ale, <u>ph</u>one
13.5	sight words

Word List

▶ Read the words from left to right. The words are new, but you have the skills to read them. Circle the words with **long e** spelled as *y*.

> copy   crispy   dries   dry   nicely   emptied   fifty   graphic   lonely   body

Define It

▶ Choose two words from the word bank. Find the meaning of the words in a dictionary. Write the definitions.

1. _____

2. _____

Circle It

▶ Read the three words in each row. Circle the two words that *end* with the same long vowel sound.

3. shy   happy   spy

4. city   safety   gym

Complete It

▶ Complete each word by filling in the blank with *wh* or *ph*. Then, write the word on the line.

5. I know how to _____isk eggs and scramble them. _____

6. Macy chats with her pals on the _____one. _____

Add It

▶ Add ending *-ly* to each base word below.

7. happy _____

8. random _____

 Use with Teaching Guide, page 542.

Silent Consonants

Name _____

Review

knot

lamb

wrap

Some letters in consonant pairs can be silent. The **k** in **kn**, the **b** in **mb**, and the **w** in **wr** are silent.

Find It

▶ Read each word. Underline the words in each row that have a **silent letter**. Then, circle the letter that is silent.

1. link   write   knife   ring
2. lamb   wrist   ramp   knob
3. knot   bank   wreck   thumb
4. branch   wrong   limb   list

Complete It

▶ **A.** Complete each word by filling in the blank with **wr** or **kn**. Then, write the whole word on the line.

5. I will ___ ite a thank you note to Wendy. _____

6. Dad uses a ___ ife to cut the sandwich. _____

7. Jess will ___ ap the gift. _____

8. There is a ___ ot in this ribbon. _____

▶ **B.** Complete each word by filling in the blank with a silent consonant.

9. The little lam ___ is very gentle.

10. ___ nock before you come in.

11. I did not get any ___ rong on the quiz.

12. The kitten is up on a lim ___ .

Open Syllables

Name

Split It

▶ Draw a line to split each word into syllables. Underline the open syllable. The first one is done for you.

1. ba|con
2. table
3. label
4. basic
5. cable
6. vacant
7. able
8. recently
9. legal
10. basis
11. decent
12. frequently

Review
basic
decent
An **open syllable** ends in a vowel. The vowel sound in an open syllable is usually long.

Write It

▶ Choose four words from Split It. Use each one in a sentence.

13. _____

14. _____

15. _____

16. _____

Choose It

▶ Choose the word with the open syllable to complete each sentence. Write it on the line.

17. Dad likes to put _____ **apple/maple** topping on his pancakes.

18. Rachel and I tell each other _____. **secrets/advice**

19. Damon _____ **just/recently** went on a trip.

20. *Un-* is a _____. **prefix/suffix**

Use with **Teaching Guide,** *page 316.*

More Open Syllables

Name _____

Split It

▶ Draw a line to split each word into syllables. Underline each open syllable. The first one is done for you.
Hint: Two other words have more than one open syllable.

1. fi|nal|ly	6. focuses
2. menu	7. unit
3. volcano	8. minus
4. omit	9. zero
5. music	10. moment

Review

menu

silent

An **open syllable** ends in a vowel. The vowel sound in an open syllable is usually long.

Circle It

▶ Read each pair of words. Then, circle the word that has an open syllable.

11. human	hundred		16. random	robots
12. seven	silent		17. minus	mistake
13. moment	magnet		18. online	omit
14. problem	pilot		19. music	muffin
15. unit	until		20. program	plastic

Write It

▶ Choose two words you circled above. Use each one in a sentence.

21. _____

22. _____

*Use with **Teaching Guide**, page 316.*

Unstressed Open Syllables

Name _____

Split It

▶ Draw a line to split each word into syllables. Underline the open syllable in each word. The first one is done for you.

1. mag|nif|i|cent
2. confidently
3. celebrate
4. selects

5. divide
6. amaze
7. politely
8. hesitate

9. habitat
10. define
11. adult
12. complicate

Review
amaze
define
The vowel sound in an **open syllable** is usually long. But when a syllable is unstressed, its vowel sound may get "clipped," or reduced to schwa.

Sort It

▶ Write the words from Split It in the correct column of the chart. One is done for you.

13. 2-syllable words	14. 3-syllable words	15. 4-syllable words
selects		

Use with **Teaching Guide,** page 324.

con-, com-

Name _____

Circle It

► Circle the word in each row that begins with *com-* or *con-*. Then, draw a line to split the circled words into syllables.

1. command   cupcake   camel

2. chopping   conflict   channel

All Mixed Up

► **A.** Unscramble the words. Write each letter on a line.

combines	command	comment	confess
confuse	consist	contracts	

3. mcondam

4. tsnocis

5. esnofcs

6. trnocastc

7. snofcue

8. scimeobn

9. mtocemn

► **B.** Write the circled letters in order. It will give you the answer to this riddle.

When you put this on, it may confuse others. They may not recognize you!

10. ___ ___ ___ ___ ___ ___ ___

Use with **Teaching Guide,** *page 532.*

Sight Words Name _____

Puzzle Fun

▶ Use words from the word bank to fill in the puzzle.

again	another	around	done	during
first	mother	pretty	soon	though

Across

3. I finished my math test. I am all _____.

4. The ribbon on the gift is very _____.

6. I get dizzy if I spin _____.

8. That game was fun. Let's play it _____!

Down

1. If we don't go _____, we will be late.

2. I call my _____ "Mom."

3. Do not chat _____ class.

5. _____ I ate an apple, I am still hungry.

6. Would you like _____ glass of milk?

7. Macy got a medal when she won _____ place.

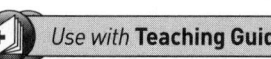

Word List

▶ Read the words from left to right. The words are new, but you have the skills to read them. Circle the words that have open syllables with a **long vowel sound**.

> aside   contacted   developing   fatal   global   items
> sequence   magnificently   units   wrote

Split It

▶ Draw a line to split the words into syllables. Underline the stressed syllable in each word.

1. aside

2. global

3. select

4. sequence

5. amaze

6. fatal

Sort It

▶ Write the words from Split It in the correct column of the chart. You may use a dictionary to help you.

7. Long Vowel Sound in First Syllable	8. Short Vowel or Schwa Sound in First Syllable

*Use with **Teaching Guide,** page 542.*

Spelling Pattern

Long *a* Vowel Team *ai* as in *train*

Name

Find It

▶ Read each word. Underline the words that have the long *a* sound you hear in *train*. Then, circle the letters that stand for that sound. The first one is done for you.

1. <u>ch(ai)n</u>   p(a)g(e)   happen   w(ai)st
2. stand   rain   tame   paint
3. brain   lamp   maze   take

Review
tr<u>ai</u>n
m<u>ai</u>l
The **vowel team** *ai* stands for the **long *a* sound** in these words.

Link It

▶ Finish each word chain. Leave *ai* in the middle. Then, add or change one letter at a time. The first one is done for you.

4. Go from **sail** to **trail**.
sail
tail
trail

5. Go from **braid** to **train**.
___
___
___

6. Go from **pail** to **plain**.
___
___
___

Sentence Solver

▶ Use words from the word bank to complete each sentence.

brain   rain   braid   train

7. Jill will _____ her hair.

8. You use your _____ to think.

9. Mom takes the _____ to her job in the city.

10. We had a picnic in the _____. My sandwich got wet!

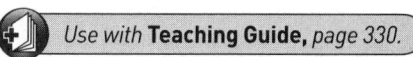

*Use with **Teaching Guide**, page 330.*

Name _____

Review
pl<u>ay</u>
tr<u>ay</u>
The **vowel team *ay*** stands for the **long *a* sound** at the ends of these words.

Find It

Underline the words in each row that have the **long *a* sound**.

1. clay   last   day

2. sang   play   mail

3. rake   stray   stamp

Sentence Solver

▶ Use words from the word bank to complete each sentence.

hay	pay	stray	way
tray	stay	sway	

4. When I tell my dog, "_____," he sits still.

5. We _____ to the music when we dance.

6. Use a _____ to bring your lunch to the table.

7. What is the best _____ to get home from here?

8. How much did you _____ for the ticket?

9. _____ is grass that is cut and dried.

10. If we find a _____ kitten, we will adopt it.

Syllable Types

Long *a* Vowel Team Syllables

Name

Split It

▶ Draw a line to split each word into syllables. Underline the syllable that has the **long *a* sound**. The first one is done for you.

1. com|<u>plain</u>
2. essay
3. explaining
4. delayed
5. contain
6. displaying
7. untrained
8. holidays
9. detail

> ### Review
>
> de<u>tail</u>
>
> <u>essay</u>
>
> Syllables with the *ai* or *ay* vowel team have a **long *a* vowel sound**. When you split a word with this pattern into syllables, keep the letters of the vowel team together.

Complete It

▶ Complete each word by filling in the blank with *ai* or *ay*. You may use a dictionary to help you.

10. afr __ d
11. del __ ed
12. tr__ ning
13. dec __ ing
14. m __ nt __ n
15. pl __ ing
16. obt __ ning
17. sw __ ing
18. br __ ded

Write It

▶ Choose four words from Complete It. Use each one in a sentence.

19. _____

20. _____

21. _____

22. _____

Name

All Mixed Up

▶ Unscramble the words from the word bank and fill in the blanks.

| science | before | question | father |
| most | work | | |

1. I call my _____ "Dad."   **htarfe**

2. Clay ate _____ of his lunch but left a little bit.   **otms**

3. We have a lab in _____ class.   **ceinesc**

4. The answer to the _____ is "Yes."   **oqtiunse**

5. I brush my teeth _____ I go to bed.   **freobe**

6. Kayla and Mason _____ in the shop.   **rowk**

Match It

▶ Draw a line from each word in Column 1 to its meaning in Column 2.

Column 1	Column 2
7. often	too
8. few	frequently
9. also	one time
10. once	not many

Use with **Teaching Guide,** *page 524.*

Series 15 Review | Name

Word List

▶ Read the words from left to right. The words are new, but you have the skills to read them. Circle the words with **two syllables**.

daytime   mailboxes   paid   playoffs   raindrops
sprained   spraying   stayed   unexplained   waiting

Define It

▶ Choose two words from the word bank. Find the meaning of the words in a dictionary. Write the definitions.

1. _____

2. _____

Build It

▶ Build words with the long *a* sound using one letter or letter pair from each box. The first one is done for you.

Beginning Letters	**Vowel Teams**	**Ending Letters**
br m pl r s spr st	ai ay	d l n ed ing

3. _____*sail*_____   6. _____   9. _____

4. _____   7. _____   10. _____

5. _____   8. _____   11. _____

*Use with **Teaching Guide,** page 542.*

Spelling Pattern

Long *o* Vowel Team
oa as in *soap*

Name _____

Review

soap

toast

The vowel team *oa* stands for the **long o sound** in these words.

Complete It

▶ Complete each word by filling in the blank with *oa*. Then, write a sentence using the word you made. The first one is done for you.

1. g_oa_l   *I made the winning goal.* _____

2. thr___t _____

3. c___st _____

4. t___st _____

5. fl___t _____

6. t___d _____

Riddle Fun

▶ **A.** Read each clue. Then, choose the word from the word bank that best answers each one. Write each letter on a line.

soak	**coach**	**coat**	**loan**	**soap**

7. Use this when you scrub your hands. __ __ __ (__)

8. You get wet when you do this. __ (__) __ __

9. When you lend cash, it is this. __ __ (__) __

10. Put this on when it is chilly. (__) __ __ __

11. One who helps you play a game. __ __ __ __ (__)

▶ **B.** Write the circled letters on the line below to find a word that tells one way you can make an egg.

12. _____

Name

Circle It

▶ Read each word. If a word has the **long *o* sound** you hear in ***flow*,** circle the letters that stand for the sound. The first one is **done for you.**

1. cr(ow)   soap   tray   rope   bike   snow
2. joke   best   glow   throat   lake   throw
3. toast   shown   loaf   gave   bowl   shy

Sentence Solver

▶ **Use words from the word bank to complete each sentence.**

crow	row	snow	slow	bowl
stow	tow	throw	shown	grown

4. Li's van got stuck in the icy _____,

   so he had to get a _____ truck.

5. Can a _____ fly for miles without stopping?

6. _____ the ball to me.

7. We can _____ the boat across the lake.

8. _____ your things in the bin on the plane.

9. My puppy has _____ so much that he does not fit in his bed.

10. Madison ate apple slices from a _____.

11. Have you _____ Jenna the bracelet you made?

12. Do you run at a fast or _____ pace?

Use with **Teaching Guide,** *page 336.*

Long *o* Vowel Team Syllables

Name

Split It

▶ Draw a line to split each word into syllables. Underline the syllable that has a **long *o* sound**. The first one is done for you. Hint: Two words have three syllables.

1. el|<u>bow</u>

2. mellow

3. sailboat

4. flowing

5. following

6. unknown

7. approaches

8. railroad

9. unloaded

All Mixed Up

▶ Read each clue. Then, unscramble each of the words.

hollow	elbow	windows	sailboat
approaches	railroad	pillows	

10. These are on a bed. _____ **wlolips**

11. Gets close. _____ **hoaprapces**

12. These are made of glass. _____ **dwsionw**

13. This is a part of your body. _____ **lobwe**

14. This has tracks for trains. _____ **aoriladr**

15. A thing that is empty inside is this. _____ **hoolwl**

16. Ride this on a lake. _____ **tlobaisa**

*Use with **Teaching Guide**, page 344.*

Sight Words | Name _____

Puzzle Fun

▶ Use the words from the word bank to fill in the puzzle.

after	choose	eight	either	favorite
four	idea	learn	none	area

Across

3. The answer to 4 + 4 is _____.

4. Mike is happy when his _____ band has a show.

5. We _____ how to multiply in math class.

7. Do you want to go bike riding before or _____ lunch?

9. We can fly kites in an open space, or _____.

Down

1. I have an _____! We can go sledding if it snows.

2. Macy will _____ the kitten she wants to take home.

3. We can _____ go shopping or go to the game. We cannot do both.

6. _____ of us got a goal, so we did not win the playoffs.

8. The answer to 2 + 2 is _____.

 *Use with **Teaching Guide,** page 524.*

Series 16 Review   Name

Series 16 Review	
16.1	soap, toast
16.2	snow, grown
16.3	knowing, railroad
16.4	sight words

Word List

▶ Read the words from left to right. The words are new, but you have the skills to read them. Circle the words with **long o** spelled *oa*. Underline the words with **long o** spelled *ow*.

> coaches   coastline   known   load   mow
> oak   owns   roads   thrown   yellow

Define It

▶ Choose four words from the word bank. Find the meaning of the words in a dictionary. Write the definitions.

1. _____

2. _____

3. _____

4. _____

Complete It

▶ Complete each word by filling in the blank with *oa* or *ow*. Then, write the whole word on the line. You may use a dictionary to help you.

5. wind____   _____

6. thr____t   _____

7. g____l   _____

8. foll____ing   _____

9. sh____n   _____

10. c____ches   _____

11. sailb____t   _____

Just for Fun

12. What might you see if the sun shines when it is snowing?

A snowbow!

Use with **Teaching Guide,** page 542.

Word Parts

Prefixes *re-, pre-*

Name _____

Circle It

▶ Circle the word in each row that has a prefix. Then, write the meaning of the word on the line. You may use a dictionary to help you. The first one is done for you.

1. present   (precut)   presses   *cut in advance*

2. repainted   rented   relaxed   _____

3. president   pretend   prepaid   _____

4. recent   rethink   rental   _____

Sentence Solver

▶ Use words from the word bank to complete each sentence.

premixed	rewrite	refilled	refresh
prejudge	recheck	prepaid	pretest

5. Mr. Jimenez gave us a _____ to see how many math problems we could do.

6. After I spilled my milk, I _____ the glass.

7. Dad _____ the muffin batter, so I can bake the muffins now.

8. José spent cash and _____ for his ticket.

9. Check your answers and then go back and _____ them.

10. I will use a new pen to _____ this note.

Write It

▶ Find the two words you did not use in Sentence Solver. Use one of them in a sentence.

11. _____

 Use with **Teaching Guide,** *page 532.*

Long *e* Vowel Team
ea as in *team*

Name

team

read

The vowel team *ea* stands for the **long e sound** in these words.

Circle It

▶ **A.** Read the words. Then, circle the words with the **long *e* sound** you hear in *team*.

1. beach   bench   left   leaf   jets   jeans
2. test   team   speak   spent   mess   desk
3. dent   deal   went   wheat   clench   dream

▶ **B.** Find and circle the words you circled in Part A. The words can be down, across, or diagonal.

```
t  x  r  m  t  e  a  m  h  j
m  s  p  s  z  w  h  e  a  t
r  s  j  r  p  r  a  q  y  h
j  j  n  c  d  e  l  e  a  f
z  e  f  u  b  e  a  c  h  d
w  q  a  l  z  g  r  k  r  r
t  u  e  n  m  l  g  c  p  e
d  h  v  l  s  f  c  e  z  a
t  c  q  j  d  e  a  l  l  m
```

Link It

▶ Finish each word chain. Add or change one letter at a time. Leave *ea* in the middle. Some are done for you.

4. Go from **deal** to **read**.	5. Go from **dream** to **scream**	6. Go from **leaf** to **clean**.
deal	_____	leaf
real	_____	_____
read	scream	_____

Use with **Teaching Guide**, page 340.

Long *e* Vowel Team
ee* as in *feet   Name

Complete It

▶ **A.** Complete each word by filling in the blank with ***ee*** or ***ea***. You may use a dictionary to help you.

1. ch_____se	**6.** l_____f	**11.** d_____p
2. wh_____t	**7.** r_____ch	**12.** dr_____m
3. kn_____	**8.** sp_____ch	**13.** scr_____n
4. scr_____m	**9.** sp_____k	**14.** fr_____
5. wh_____l	**10.** sp_____d	

<table>
<tr><td colspan="1">**Review**</td></tr>
<tr><td>

f<u>ee</u>t

t<u>ee</u>n

The vowel team *ee* stands for the **long e sound** in these words.
</td></tr>
</table>

▶ **B.** Use the words you made with ***ee*** in Part A to complete each sentence.

15. How _____ is the lake? Can we swim in it?

16. Is the show _____, or do we have to pay?

17. Lin gave a _____ when she won the contest.

18. Would you like _____ on your sandwich?

19. We will see the program on a big _____ TV.

20. Did you scrape your _____ when you fell?

21. Justin has to fix the wagon _____.

22. Molly rides a ten-_____ bike.

*Use with **Teaching Guide,** page 340.*

Name

Sort It

▶ Read the words in the word bank. Find the letters that stand for the **long e sound** you hear in *piece*. Write each word in the correct column. One is done for you.

wheel	niece	reach	shield	seek
team	yield	feet	scream	beach
chief	creek			

1. long e spelled *ea*	2. long e spelled *ee*	3. long e spelled *ie*
_____	*wheel*	_____
_____	_____	_____
_____	_____	_____
_____	_____	_____

Write It

▶ Choose one word from each column in Sort It. Use each one in a sentence.

4. _____

5. _____

6. _____

Long *e* Vowel Team Syllables

Name _____

Review

freedom

eagles

Syllables with the *ee* or *ea* vowel teams have a **long e sound**.

Split It

▶ Draw a line to split each word into syllables. Underline the syllable that has a **long e vowel team**. Hint: One word has three syllables.

1. nineteen
2. eagles
3. defeated
4. reason
5. greeting
6. sixteen
7. decrease
8. ideal
9. asleep

Complete It

▶ Complete each word by filling in the blank with *ea* or *ee*. You may use a dictionary to help you. Then, write a sentence with the word you made. The first one is done for you.

10. degr _ee_   *When Alex finishes college, he will have a degree.*

11. m____ning _____

12. ninet____n _____

13. car____r _____

14. ben____th _____

15. agr____ _____

Name _____

Sentence Solver

▶ Use words from the word bank to complete each sentence.

become	better	bought	brought	gone
group	nothing	school	tomorrow	usual

1. The plain iced tea is good, but the peach tea is _____.

2. I take six classes at _____.

3. Sammy likes to travel with a _____. He does not like to go by himself.

4. I had a little cash, so I _____ a gift for Julia.

5. My dog ate all the meat in his dish. There is _____ left!

6. The word _____ is related to the word *bring*.

7. I did not have time to jog yesterday, but I will _____.

8. Mom went on a trip for work. She will be _____ for three days.

9. My cat always takes a nap on the red pillow. It is his _____ place to sleep.

10. If I make lunch more often, I could _____ a talented chef!

Match It

▶ Draw a line from each word in Column 1 to its meaning in Column 2.

Column 1	Column 2
11. gone	paid for
12. school	left
13. bought	place with classes

Use with **Teaching Guide,** *page 524.*

Series 17 Review   Name

Series 17 Review

17.1	replay, pretest
17.2	team, read
17.3	feet, teen
17.4	shield, chief
17.5	freedom, eagles
17.6	sight words

Word List

▶ Read the words from left to right. The words are new, but you have the skills to read them. Circle the word that has **three syllables**.

achieve belief decreasing green neatly

pregame reading repaid replace teenage

Sort It

▶ Each word in the word bank has a syllable with a long *a* vowel team or a long *e* vowel team. Read each word. Then, write it in the correct column of the chart. One is done for you.

achieve   complain   delayed   belief   explaining
reading   neatly   obtaining   decreasing   afraid

1. Long *a* Vowel Team	2. Long *e* Vowel Team
	achieve

Use with **Teaching Guide,** page 542.

Name _____

Circle It

▶ Read each word. If a word has the **long *i* sound** you hear in *light*, circle the letters that stand for the sound. The first one is done for you.

Review
<u>light</u>
br<u>igh</u>t
The letters *-igh* stand for the **long *i* sound** in these words.

1. fl(igh)t   fit   bite   my   lift   sight
2. cry   slight   mixed   mile   night   twin
3. nine   tripped   fright   try   high   while

Complete It

▶ **A.** Complete each word by filling in the blank with *-igh* or *y*. Then, write the word on the line. You may use a dictionary to help you.

4. br_____t   _____

5. s_____   _____

6. fl_____   _____

7. t_____t   _____

8. sh_____   _____

9. cr_____   _____

10. l_____t   _____

▶ **B.** Find the words you made with *-igh*. Use each one in a sentence.

11. _____

12. _____

13. _____

14. _____

 Use with **Teaching Guide,** *page 350.*

Other Long Vowel Spellings

Name _____

Build It

▶ Add each letter or letter pair to the letters in the box. If it forms a real word, write it on the line. You may use a dictionary to help you.

b c g j qu	1. _____
-olt	2. _____
	3. _____

b d f m s	4. _____
-ind	5. _____
	6. _____

| b h m st w | 7. _____ |
| **-ild** | 8. _____ |

c d g s sc	9. _____
-old	10. _____
	11. _____
	12. _____

f r str t v	13. _____
-oll	14. _____
	15. _____

Review

bolt

mind

mild

gold

roll

Each of these words has a **long vowel sound**.

*Use with **Teaching Guide**, page 354.*

Analyzing Word Structure

Name

Mark It

▶ Read each word. Underline the **prefix**. Circle the **suffix** or **word ending**. Then, write the **base word** on the line. The first one is done for you.

1. <u>de</u>compos(ing)   *compose*
2. uncomplicated   _____
3. rewriting   _____
4. unhappiness   _____
5. unplugged   _____
6. defrosted   _____
7. unpacking   _____

Choose It

▶ Choose the correct form of each word and write it on the line.

8. Are you _____ the frozen meat?
 defrost, defrosting, defrosted

9. My baseball team has not lost a single game. We are _____.
 defeat, undefeated, defeated

10. I have an _____ supply of pencils. Help yourself!
 unlimited, limit, limiting

11. Lissa is _____ the clues in the puzzle.
 scramble, unscramble, unscrambling

12. Josh waited for the plane to land, and then he _____ his seatbelt.   **buckle, unbuckled, unbuckling**

*Use with **Teaching Guide**, page 376.*

Name

Find It

▶ Follow the directions to find the word that means "confident."

toward	special	sure	direction
pull	country	build	

1. Cross out the word with three syllables and write it here. _____

2. Cross out the word that names a place and write it here. _____

3. Cross out the word that means "to make" and write it here. _____

4. Cross out the word that starts with an *s*- blend and write it here.

_____

5. Cross out the word that can mean "to tug" and write it here. _____

6. Cross out the word that tells a direction and write it here. _____

7. Write the word that is left over and that means "confident." _____

Sentence Solver

▶ **Use words from the word bank to complete each sentence.**

world	ready	walk

8. Should we _____ to school or take the bus?

9. Is Misha _____ to take the test?

10. The globe shows all the places on our planet, or _____ .

Use with **Teaching Guide,** page 524.

Word List

Series 18 Review
18.1 light, bright
18.2 bolt, mind, mild, gold, roll
18.3 defrosted, unwillingness
18.4 sight words

▶ Read the words from left to right. The words are new, but you have the skills to read them. Circle six words that have a **long vowel sound**.

child   fight   folded   holding   golden   remodeling

replaying   right   unexpected   unlocked

Define It

▶ Choose two words from the word bank. Find the meaning of the words in a dictionary. Write the definitions.

1. _____

2. _____

Word Search

▶ Circle the words in the puzzle. The words can be down or across.

child   golden   replaying   right   unexpected

```
s  q  c  p  p  y  w  t  c  n
u  n  e  x  p  e  c  t  e  d
y  r  e  p  l  a  y  i  n  g
b  t  k  n  f  p  u  a  d  r
r  h  u  z  p  c  c  d  r  i
t  q  c  y  j  z  z  m  e  g
z  i  o  c  h  i  l  d  l  h
d  m  g  o  l  d  e  n  i  t
```

Use with **Teaching Guide,** page 542.

Spelling Pattern

ar as in *cart*

Name _____

List It

▶ Read the words in the word bank. Then, write the words that have the *ar* sound as in *star* on the lines below.

mail	art	dark	play	large
shark	snake	park	card	cage

Review

cart

star

When letter *r* follows a vowel, the sound of the vowel may change.

1. _____   4. _____

2. _____   5. _____

3. _____   6. _____

Sentence Solver

▶ Choose words you wrote above to complete each sentence.

7. A _____ can see well under water.

8. Alex sent me a thank-you _____ for the gift.

9. That dog is _____. He will not fit in this tiny car!

10. We play catch in the _____ .

11. I like to paint in _____ class.

12. A flashlight can help you see in the _____ .

Does It Rhyme?

▶ Read each word pair. Write *Yes* if the words rhyme. Write *No* if they do not rhyme. Then, write a new rhyming word for the word that is underlined. The first one is done for you.

Word Pair	Rhyme?	New Rhyme
13. <u>cart</u> cat	*no*	*part*
14. shark <u>park</u>	_____	_____
15. <u>star</u> far	_____	_____
16. last <u>charge</u>	_____	_____

 Use with **Teaching Guide**, *page 358.*

Syllables with *ar*

Name

Split It

▶ Draw a line to split each word into syllables. Underline the syllable that has a vowel followed by *r*.

1. apartment
2. partly
3. garlic
4. enlarge
5. charcoal
6. target
7. parka
8. alarming
9. discarded
10. market
11. gardens
12. depart

Review

artist

party

When a syllable has a vowel followed by letter *r*, the *r* may change the vowel sound.

All Mixed Up

▶ Unscramble each word to match a word in the word bank and to complete each sentence.

| party | depart | artist | market | participate |

13. The _____ made a beautiful painting. **tstira**

14. Did you invite the whole class to the _____? **rytpa**

15. We will leave, or _____, at six o'clock. **rdatep**

16. Jasmin will take part, or _____, in the meeting. **cpiaettapri**

17. Dad got apples and plums at the _____. **kterma**

Use with **Teaching Guide**, page 382.

Name

Complete It

▶ Complete each word by filling in the blank with *er*, *ir*, or *ur*. You may use a dictionary to help you.

> **Review**
>
> **germ**
>
> **bird**
>
> **hurt**
>
> When letter *r* follows a vowel, the sound of the vowel may change.

1. The bike rack is by the c_____b.

2. Darlene fell off her bike, but she did not

   h_____t h_____self.

3. Do you know how to s_____f a big wave?

4. A complete sentence has a noun and a v_____b.

5. The b_____d rested on a branch and sang a song.

6. Scrub your hands with soap to get rid of g_____ms.

7. Dad was not happy when we tracked d_____t on the rug.

8. I will st_____the pancake mix.

Write It

▶ Choose four words from Complete It. Use each word in a sentence.

9. _____

10. _____

11. _____

12. _____

 Use with **Teaching Guide,** *page 362.*

Syllables with *er*, *ir*, *ur*

Name

Split It

▶ **A.** Draw a line to split each word into syllables. Underline the syllable that has *er*, *ir*, or *ur*.

1. computer
2. disturb
3. exercises

4. surprise
5. pattern
6. return

7. thirsty
8. circles
9. percent

Review
concern
circles
surprise

When a syllable has a vowel followed by letter *r*, the *r* may change the vowel sound.

▶ **B.** Write the answer to each question about the words in Part A.

10. Which word has the most syllables? _____

11. How many syllables does it have? _____

12. Which words have syllables with *er*? _____

_____ _____ _____

13. Which words have syllables with *ir*?

_____ _____

14. Which words have syllables with *ur*? _____

_____ _____

Write It

▶ Choose two words from Split It. Use each one in a sentence.

15. _____

16. _____

Use with **Teaching Guide,** *page 382.*

Name

Find It

▶ Read each word. Underline the words that have letters that stand for the *sh* sound you hear in *fiction*.

1. option	sense	official
2. surf	motion	patience
3. facial	station	little
4. depart	social	lotion
5. glacier	attention	reason

Review

official

lotion

The letters *ti* and *ci* can stand for the same sound as the digraph *sh*.

Sort It

▶ Write the words you underlined in Find It in the correct column of the chart.

6. *sh* sound spelled *ti*	7. *sh* sound spelled *ci*

Write It

▶ Choose three words from Sort It. Use each one in a sentence.

8. _____

9. _____

10. _____

*Use with **Teaching Guide,** page 366.*

Sight Words   Name _____

Sentence Solver

▶ **A.** Use words from the word bank to complete each sentence.

accept	certain	early	enough	eye
heard	listen	love	people	woman

1. If we get to the show _____ , we will not have to wait in line.

2. Did you _____ to the new song?

3. Dad _____ the baby crying, so he got her a bottle.

4. I _____ playing soccer. It is my favorite thing to do!

5. Is there _____ milk left for all of us?

▶ **B.** Find the words that you did not use in Part A. Use two of the words in a sentence.

6. _____

7. _____

Match It

▶ Draw a line from each word in Column 1 to its meaning in Column 2.

Column 1	Column 2
8. early	sure
9. eye	like very much
10. love	humans
11. people	you see with this
12. certain	not late

Use with **Teaching Guide,** *page 524.*

Name

Word List

▶ Read the words from left to right. The words are new, but you have the skills to read them. Circle the words with *ar* as in *star*.

nonfiction impatient hard harvest nation

number parked partner swirling turn

Series 19 Review

19.1	cart, star
19.2	artist, party
19.3	germ, bird, hurt
19.4	concern, circles, surprise
19.5	official, lotion
19.6	sight words

Define It

Choose three words from the word bank. Find the meaning of the words in a dictionary. Write the definitions.

1. _____

2. _____

3. _____

Circle It

▶ Circle the two words in each row that have the same vowel sound. The first one is done for you.

4. (turn)   fuse   (burn)
5. hard   card   cake
6. swirling   twirling   sighing
7. germ   harm   term
8. dirt   shirt   pier
9. shark   braid   dark

Just for Fun

▶ Say this tongue twister five times fast!

10. Twelve twins twirled twelve twigs.

 *Use with **Teaching Guide**, page 542.*

Name _____

Complete It

► Complete each word by filling in the blank with *or* or *ore*. You may use a dictionary to help you.

1. c_____d
2. st_____
3. t_____ch

4. f_____ce
5. n_____th
6. sc_____

7. s_____
8. sp_____t
9. st_____m

Review

sp<u>or</u>t

st<u>ore</u>

When letter *r* follows a vowel, the sound of the vowel may change.

Write It

► Choose two words from Complete It. Use each one in a sentence.

10. _____

11. _____

Link It

► Finish each word chain. Add or change one letter at a time.

12. Go from
turn to **born**.

_____turn_____

_____

_____

_____

13. Go from
mare to **store**.

_____mare_____

_____

_____sore_____

_____

14. Go from
storm to **score**.

_____storm_____

_____

_____

_____

*Use with **Teaching Guide,** page 372.*

Syllables with *or, ore*

Name _____

Split It

▶ Draw a line to split each word into syllables. Underline the syllable that has *or* or *ore*.

1. corner
2. ignore
3. organize
4. portion

5. explore
6. important
7. prerecording
8. performed

9. restore
10. normal
11. adore
12. incorrectly

Sort It

▶ Write the words from Split It in the correct column of the chart.

13. 2-syllable words	14. 3-syllable words	15. 4-syllable words

Write It

▶ Choose one word from each column in Sort It. Use each one in a sentence.

16. _____

17. _____

18. _____

 Use with **Teaching Guide,** *page 382.*

Word Parts

Suffixes -er, -or

Name

Match It

▶ Write the word from the word bank that matches each clue. The first one is done for you.

doctor	driver	painter	performers
reporter	runners	teacher	swimmer

Review

<u>teacher</u>

<u>doctor</u>

The suffixes -er and -or in these words show that they are related to things that people do.

1. They compete in races. ___*runners*___

2. This person may use a brush. _____

3. This person speaks to a class. _____

4. This person might jump in a lake. _____

5. This person can help when you feel ill. _____

6. They may sing or dance on a stage. _____

7. This person uses a car. _____

8. This person may tell about current events. _____

All Mixed Up

▶ Unscramble the words from the word bank to answer each riddle.

speaker	inventor	writer	trainer	beginner	director

9. I make new things. Who am I? **nverotni** _____

10. I may give speeches. Who am I? **psrekae** _____

11. I can type stories on a computer. Who am I? **rtewir** _____

12. I am doing something for the first time. Who am I? **gnbneire** _____

13. I can teach a dog new tricks. Who am I? **reanrti** _____

14. I am in charge of making films. Who am I? **toridrec** _____

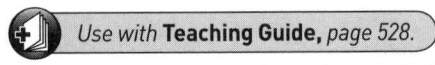 *Use with* **Teaching Guide,** *page 528.*

Suffixes *-er, -est*

Name

Add It

▶ Add *-er* or *-est* to each base word. Write the new word on the line.

1. My cat has _____ fur than my dog. **soft**

2. Anna is the _____ runner in our class. **quick**

3. Jess has three books. She wants to read the

_____ one! **thick**

4. Lee's desk is _____ than mine. **clean**

Review

quicker

quickest

Use the suffix *-er* to compare two people or things. Use the suffix *-est* to compare more than two people or things.

Complete It

▶ Complete the chart. The first one is done for you.

Base Word	-er	-est
5. chilly	chillier	chilliest
6.	colder	
7. high		highest
8. lucky		luckiest
9.	softer	
10.		cleanest
11. thick		
12.	smarter	
13. sunny	sunnier	
14. quick		
15.	deeper	
16. wide		

Use with **Teaching Guide,** *page 528.*

air* as in *chair*, *are* as in *share*, *ear* as in *bear

Name _____

Review
chair
share
bear
Letter *r* changes the vowel sound in these words.

Add It

▶ Add *air*, *are*, or *ear* to each beginning letter to make a word. You may use a dictionary for help. Hint: Some of the words sound the same, but have different spellings and meanings.

1. b_____   5. b_____   9. ch_____

2. p_____   6. p_____   10. sc_____

3. sh_____   7. sp_____   11. squ_____

4. st_____   8. st_____   12. w_____

Write It

▶ Choose two words from Add It. Use each one in a sentence.

13. _____

14. _____

Choose It

▶ **Homophones** are words that sound the same but have different spellings and meanings. Choose the correct homophone for each sentence. Write it on the line.

15. A _____ looks like a rabbit. **hare, hair**

16. Dominic needs a new _____ of pants. **pare, pair, pear**

17. Go up the _____ and wait for me. **stares, stairs**

18. Lukas gave me a _____ for a snack. **pare, pair, pear**

19. Did you see a _____ on your hike? **bare, bear**

20. Rosa wants to cut her _____ short. **hare, hair**

Use with **Teaching Guide,** *page 378.*

Name

Review

upstairs

compare

The letter *r* changes the vowel sound in the second syllable of these words.

Split It

▶ Draw a line to split each word into syllables. Underline the syllable that has *air* or *are*.

1. awareness
2. careless
3. despair
4. repairing

5. barely
6. compare
7. prepare
8. software

9. unfairly
10. dairy
11. rarely
12. upstairs

Match It

▶ Draw a line from the syllable on the left to a syllable on the right to make a word.

13. de   less
14. pre   spair
15. soft   stairs
16. up   ware
17. care   pare

Write It

▶ Read the words you made in Match It. Use each one in a sentence.

18. _____

19. _____

20. _____

21. _____

22. _____

Use with **Teaching Guide,** *page 382.*

Name _____

Word List

▶ Read the words from left to right. The words are new, but you have the skills to read them. Circle the words with *are*. Underline the words with *air*.

> airfare   farewell   former   hotter   hottest
>
> sailor   sorting   supported   tore   unfair

Series 20 Review

20.1	sport, store
20.2	report, adore
20.3	teacher, doctor
20.4	quicker, quickest
20.5	chair, share, bear
20.6	upstairs, compare

Define It

▶ Choose four words from the word bank. Find the meaning of the words in a dictionary. Write the definitions.

1. _____

2. _____

3. _____

4. _____

Circle It

▶ Circle the words in each row that have a suffix. Then, underline the suffix.

5.	director	store	teacher
6.	cord	colder	chilliest
7.	trainer	writer	software
8.	dairy	darker	thickest

Just for Fun

▶ Say this tongue twister five times fast!

9. A big brown bug bit a big brown bear.

 *Use with **Teaching Guide**, page 542.*

Name

Find It

▶ Read each word. Underline the words that have the vowel sound you hear in *coin* and *toy*. Then, circle the letters that stand for the vowel sound you hear in *coin* and *toy*. The first one is started for you.

1. sort	s**oy**	soil	box	boy	bone
2. coin	cot	choice	top	tone	toy
3. note	noise	notch	joy	point	pole

> ### Review
>
> **coin**
>
> **toy**
>
> The letters *oi* and *oy* in these words stand for a gliding vowel sound.

Complete It

▶ Complete each word by filling in the blank with *oi* or *oy*. You may use a dictionary to help you.

4. b＿＿＿   **7.** m＿＿＿st   **10.** p＿＿＿nt

5. s＿＿＿l   **8.** j＿＿＿   **11.** v＿＿＿ce

6. n＿＿＿se   **9.** ch＿＿＿ce   **12.** t＿＿＿

Write It

▶ Choose four words from Complete It. Use each one in a sentence.

13. ＿＿＿＿＿＿＿＿＿＿＿＿＿＿＿＿＿＿＿＿＿＿＿＿＿＿＿＿＿＿

14. ＿＿＿＿＿＿＿＿＿＿＿＿＿＿＿＿＿＿＿＿＿＿＿＿＿＿＿＿＿＿

15. ＿＿＿＿＿＿＿＿＿＿＿＿＿＿＿＿＿＿＿＿＿＿＿＿＿＿＿＿＿＿

16. ＿＿＿＿＿＿＿＿＿＿＿＿＿＿＿＿＿＿＿＿＿＿＿＿＿＿＿＿＿＿

*Use with **Teaching Guide,** page 386.*

Syllables with *oi, oy*

Name _____

Split It

▶ Draw a line to split each word into syllables. Underline the syllable that has the vowel sound you hear in *coin* and *toy*.

1. annoy
2. destroy
3. loyal
4. poison

5. appointed
6. disappoint
7. noisy
8. rejoice

9. avoid
10. employment
11. ointment
12. royal

Complete It

▶ Complete each word by filling in the blank with *oi* or *oy*. You may use a dictionary to help you.

13. I am really enj_____ing my summer vacation.

14. The dog next door is very n_____sy at night.

15. The hikers were told to av_____d the p_____son ivy.

16. I will rej_____ce when I get my braces off!

17. The leader was app_____nted by a group of

    l_____al followers.

18. My sister wants to find empl_____ment as a pet sitter.

19. If you don't give the cat a treat, it will disapp_____nt her.

20. You can use _____ntment to heal the scrape on your leg.

Use with Teaching Guide, page 390.

Name _____

Review

cloud

owl

The letters *ou* and *ow* in these words stand for a gliding vowel sound.

Build It

▶ Build words with the vowel sound you hear in the words *cloud* and *owl.* Use one letter or letter pair from each box. The first one is done for you.

Beginning Letters	Vowel Teams	Ending Letters
cl cr gr m s sc sh	ou ow	d l n t th

1. _cloud_

2. _____

3. _____

4. _____

5. _____

6. _____

7. _____

8. _____

9. _____

All Mixed Up

▶ Unscramble each of the words from the word bank to answer the riddles.

mouth   crowd   growl   south   cloud

10. I am part of your face. What am I? _____ **umoht**

11. Find me in the sky. What am I? _____ **ludoc**

12. I am a noise a dog might make. What am I? _____ **wgolr**

13. I am the opposite of north. What am I? _____ **ushto**

14. I am a large group. What am I? _____ **wcdro**

Use with **Teaching Guide,** *page 394.*

Name _____

Split It

▶ Draw a line to split each word into syllables. Underline the syllable that has the vowel sound you hear in *cloud* and *owl*.

1. account
2. download
3. shower

4. announces
5. flowers
6. tower

7. browser
8. powerful
9. workout

Sentence Solver

▶ **A.** Use words from the word bank to complete each sentence. Write each letter on a line.

outline	amount	shower	cloudy
account	grouchy	tower	aloud

10. When the sun doesn't shine, it is ___ ___ ___ ___( )___ .

11. Make an ___ ___ ___ ___( )___ ___ of the text when you study for a test.

12. I take a ( )___ ___ ___ ___ ___ after soccer practice.

13. You can save cash in a bank ___( )___ ___ ___ ___ ___ .

14. First, read the text silently. Then, read it ___ ___( )___ ___ .

15. When I don't get much sleep, I feel ___ ___ ___( )___ ___ ___ .

16. What is the ___ ___ ___ ___( )___ of energy produced by the sun?

17. The castle has a tall ( )___ ___ ___ ___ .

▶ **B.** Write the circled letters in order. It will give you the answer to this clue.

If you get this when you shop, it will save you some cash.

18. ___ ___ ___ ___ ___ ___ ___ ___

Sight Words

Name

Puzzle Fun

▶ Use words from the word bank to fill in the puzzle.

beautiful	earth	head	health	money
schedule	ancient	touch	warm	water

Across

5. Dr. Landis found an _____ coin. It is a thousand years old!

7. Use a calendar to keep track of your _____.

10. Mom planted seeds in the soil, or _____.

Down

1. Your painting is _____! You did a fantastic job.

2. Do not _____ the objects in the gallery.

3. Have a glass of _____ if you are thirsty.

4. It gets very _____ and humid here in the summer.

6. I am saving my _____ to get concert tickets.

8. In _____ class, we learn how to care for our bodies.

9. A cap will keep your _____ from getting cold.

Use with **Teaching Guide,** page 524.

Name _____

Series 21 Review

21.1	coin, toy
21.2	rejoice, loyal
21.3	cloud, owl
21.4	aloud, flowers
21.5	sight words

Word List

▶ Read the words from left to right. The words are new, but you have the skills to read them. Circle the words that have two syllables.

appointments background broiling brown compound
count downtown employer found joined

Define It

▶ Choose two words from the word bank. Find the meaning of the words in a dictionary. Write the definitions.

1. _____

2. _____

Complete It

▶ Complete each word by filling in the blank with a vowel team from the box. You may use a dictionary to help you.

oi   oy   ou   ow

3. Geese fly s_____th in the winter.

4. The kitten likes to play with his t_____.

5. The singer has a beautiful v_____ce.

6. My little sister saw a cl_____n at the circus.

Just for Fun

▶ Say this tongue twister five times fast!

7. A noisy noise annoys an oyster.

Use with Teaching Guide, page 542.

Name

Build It

▶ Build new words by adding suffixes to the base words. Write each word on the line.

1. joy + ful = _____

2. fear + less = _____

3. spot + less = _____

4. force + ful = _____

5. pain + less = _____

6. cheer + ful = _____

> ### Review
>
> harmless
>
> careful
>
> • A **suffix** is a word part added at the end of a base word to change its meaning.
> • The suffix *-less* means "without."
> • The suffix *-ful* means "full of" or "great."

Add It

▶ Add *-less* or *-ful* to each underlined word. Then, write the new word on the line. The first one is done for you.

7. The dog has a loud bark, but it is gentle and <u>harm</u> *less* .

harmless

8. Be <u>care</u> _____ when you walk on the ice, so you don't slip. _____

9. A backpack is <u>use</u> _____ when you have a lot to carry. _____

10. Simon is talking on a <u>cord</u> _____ phone. _____

11. Don't be <u>waste</u> _____! Recycle paper. _____

12. I feel happy and <u>joy</u> _____! _____

Use with **Teaching Guide,** *page 528.*

Spelling Pattern

oo as in *moon*, *ew* as in *chew*, *u_e* as in *tube*

Name

Build It

▶ Fill in each blank with a letter or letter pair from the box. Then, write the word you built on the line. One is done for you.

b   c   fl   kn   l   m   n   pr   t   thr   ch   f

1. _t_ u _n_ e ___tune___	4. ___ ew _____	7. ___ oo ___ _____
2. ___ u ___ e _____	5. ___ ew _____	8. ___ oo ___ _____
3. ___ u ___ e _____	6. ___ ew _____	9. ___ oo ___ _____

Review

boot

news

tube

- The *oo* spelling usually appears in the middle of a word.
- The *ew* spelling usually appears at the end of a syllable or word.
- The letters *u _ consonant_e* can stand for the long *u* sound as in *cube*, but they can also stand for the sound you hear in *tube*.

Write It

▶ Choose five words from Build It. Use each one in a sentence.

10. _____

11. _____

12. _____

13. _____

14. _____

Use with Teaching Guide, page 404.

Syllables with *oo, ew, u_e*

Name

Split It

▶ Draw a line to split each word into syllables. Underline the syllable that has the vowel sound you hear in the words *boot* and *new*.

1. afternoon
2. pollute
3. toolbar
4. loosen
5. newspaper
6. noodles
7. include
8. gloomy
9. costume
10. cashews
11. renew
12. cartoons

Review

cartoons

renew

costume

These words have syllables with the same vowel sound spelled three different ways.

Complete It

▶ Complete each word by filling in the blank with a vowel team from the box. You may use a dictionary to help you.

| oo | ew |

13. Cash_____s are tasty nuts.

14. It's time to ren_____ my library card.

15. The rainy day started dark and gl_____my.

16. I saw the ad in the n_____spaper.

17. Emma likes eating n_____dles.

18. Jason likes to watch cart_____ns.

19. My little sister likes to try on Mom's rings and j_____els.

20. I'm going to play tennis this aftern_____n.

*Use with **Teaching Guide**, page 408.*

Sight Words   Name _____

Find It

▶ A **synonym** is a word that means the same thing as another word. An **antonym** is a word that means the **opposite**. Find the synonym or antonym that completes each sentence.

| language | picture | buy | young | carry |

1. An antonym of *sell* is _____.

2. A synonym of *lift* is _____.

3. An antonym of *old* is _____.

4. A synonym of *speech* is _____.

5. A synonym of *painting* is _____.

Sentence Solver

▶ Use words from the word bank to complete each sentence in the paragraph.

| buy | picture | clothes | measure |
| instead | neighbor | busy |

6. Jen's next-door _____ has some jeans and other

_____ to sell. Jen will _____ these things, but

she will not pay cash. _____, she will trade a

_____ that she drew.

Write It

▶ Find the words you did not use in Sentence Solver. Use each one in a sentence.

7. _____

8. _____

 *Use with **Teaching Guide**, page 524.*

Name

Word List

► Read the words from left to right. The words are new, but you have the skills to read them. Circle the words that have a suffix or ending.

Series 22 Review	
22.1	harmless, careful
22.2	boot, news, tube
22.3	cartoons, renew, costume
22.4	sight words

cooling   crew   endless   graceful   helpless   hopefully
newscaster   renewing   scooter   sunroof

Define It

► Choose four words from the word bank. Find the meaning of the words in a dictionary. Write the definitions.

1. _____

2. _____

3. _____

4. _____

Circle It

► Circle the words in each row that have the same vowel sound as *boot* and *new*.

5. crew	creep	cool
6. shampoo	sunroof	shower
7. tame	tune	tube

Just for Fun

► Say this tongue twister five times fast!

8. Drew knew no new news.

 Use with **Teaching Guide,** page 542.

Name _____

Does It Rhyme?

▶ Read each word pair. Write **Yes** if the words rhyme. Write **No** if they do not rhyme. Then, write a new rhyming word for the word that is underlined. The first one is done for you.

Review

book

push

These words have a vowel sound that is not long or short.

Word Pair		Rhyme?	New Rhyme
1. book	hook	*yes*	*look*
2. push	lash	_____	_____
3. stood	hood	_____	_____
4. tank	shook	_____	_____
5. pull	mail	_____	_____
6. land	wood	_____	_____

All Mixed Up

▶ **A.** Unscramble the words from the word bank. Write each letter on a line.

> bush   wood   shook   cook   wool

7. I like to help my dad (__) __ __ __ dinner. **koco**

8. The past tense of "shake" is __ __ (__) __ __. **hosko**

9. Mom planted a __ (__) __ __ in the garden. **subh**

10. __ __ __ (__) comes from sheep. **lowo**

11. __ __ __ (__) comes from trees. **dowo**

▶ **B.** Write the circled letters in order. It will give you the answer to this riddle.

This word rhymes with *wood*, but it does not have *oo* in the middle.

12. __ __ __ __ __

 Use with Teaching Guide, page 412.

Syllables with *oo, u*

Name

Split it

▶ Draw a line to split each word into syllables. Underline the syllable that has the vowel sound you hear in ***book*** and ***put***.

1. rookie
2. mistook
3. bushes

4. input
5. outlook
6. textbook

7. footsteps
8. fulfilling
9. wooden

> ### Review
>
> notebook
>
> pushing
>
> These words have syllables with a vowel sound that is not long or short.

Circle It

▶ Read each pair of words. Then, circle the word that has a syllable with the same vowel sound you hear in ***book*** and ***put***.

10. until   uncooked
11. wooden   winter
12. compose   looking

13. crooked   pocket
14. pollute   pushing
15. childhood   cashew

Write It

▶ Find the words you circled above. Use each one in a sentence.

16. _____

17. _____

18. _____

19. _____

20. _____

21. _____

 Use with **Teaching Guide**, *page 416.*

Spelling Pattern

aw as in *yawn*, *au* as in *launch*, *a* as in *ball*

Name _____

Find It

▶ Read each word. Underline the words that have the vowel sound you hear in *yawn*. Then, circle the letters that stand for the vowel sound you hear in *yawn*. The first one is started for you.

1. bank   ch(a)lk   paw   chair   yard   vault
2. mall   stare   fault   rain   straw   gray
3. salt   clay   launch   star   pair   ball

Write It

▶ Choose two words from Find It. Use each one in a sentence.

4. _____

5. _____

Word Search

▶ Circle the words. The words can be down, across, or diagonal.

ball	draw	fault
launch	law	taunt
vault	yawn	

```
b  o  l  a  w  d  k  o  y
z  a  u  y  y  q  w  t  k
q  e  l  q  o  a  v  a  u
d  w  m  l  z  t  w  u  d
r  v  v  a  u  l  t  n  f
a  h  l  u  w  i  m  t  b
w  k  j  r  m  f  j  u  p
y  f  a  u  l  t  z  a  z
i  r  w  l  a  u  n  c  h
```

 Use with **Teaching Guide**, *page 420.*

Name

Split It

▶ Draw a line to split each word into syllables. Underline the syllable that has the vowel sound you hear in *yawn*.

1. rainfall
2. caution
3. flawless

4. saucer
5. baseball
6. author

7. awful
8. withdraw
9. uninstall

Review

f<u>la</u>wless

app<u>lau</u>ding

b<u>a</u>sketball

These words have syllables with the same vowel sound spelled three different ways.

Complete It

▶ Read each clue. Then, complete each word by filling in the blank with a vowel or vowel team from the box. You may use a dictionary to help you.

a	aw	au

10. Clapping: appl_____ding

11. A person who may work with a judge: l_____yer

12. An actor has this before getting a part: _____dition

13. A game: basketb_____ll

14. You can put a teacup on this: s_____cer

15. Having no mistakes: fl_____less

16. A person who uses a phone: c_____ller

17. Very bad: _____ful

18. Take a program off a computer: uninst_____ll

Use with **Teaching Guide,** *page 424.*

Name

Word List

▶ Read the words from left to right. The words are new, but you have the skills to read them. Circle the words that have a syllable with the vowel sound you hear in **push**.

> autograph barefoot bookmarks causes
> dawn falling fully recall

<table>
<tr><td colspan="2">**Series 23 Review**</td></tr>
<tr><td>23.1</td><td>book, push</td></tr>
<tr><td>23.2</td><td>notebook, pushing</td></tr>
<tr><td>23.3</td><td>yawn, launch, ball</td></tr>
<tr><td>23.4</td><td>flawless, applauding, basketball</td></tr>
</table>

Define It

▶ Choose four words from the word bank. Find the meaning of the words in a dictionary. Write the definitions.

1. _____

2. _____

3. _____

4. _____

Sort It

▶ Write each word from the word bank in the correct column of the chart.

> barefoot dawn causes bookmarks
> fully recall autograph looking

5. Syllable with Vowel Sound in **book, push**	**6.** Syllable with Vowel Sound in **yawn, launch, ball**

*Use with **Teaching Guide**, page 542.*

Word Parts

Prefixes
mid-, sub-

Name _____

Review

midnight

subzero

- A **prefix** is a word part added at the beginning of a base word to change its meaning.
- The prefix *mid-* means "being in the middle."
- The prefix *sub-* means "under" or "below."

Circle It

▶ Circle the word in each row that has a prefix. Then, write the meaning of the word on the line. The first one is done for you.

1. (subzero)   saucer   shampoo   *below zero*

2. mouth   midwinter   middle   _____

3. sudden   shower   subtotal   _____

4. midtown   model   magnet   _____

True or False

▶ Read each sentence. If it is true, circle *T*. If it is false, circle *F*.

5. Sunday is a day that is **midweek**.   T   F

6. **Suburbs** are areas in the middle of cities.   T   F

7. Divers can **submerge** to look at fish.   T   F

8. **Midnight** is the middle of the day.   T   F

9. **Subways** are below the ground.   T   F

10. **Midpoint** is the middle of a line.   T   F

Write It

▶ Choose two of the words in bold print from True or False. Use each one in a sentence.

11. _____

12. _____

*Use with **Teaching Guide**, page 532.*

Word Parts

Prefixes
dis-, mis-

Name

Match It

▶ Add a prefix from Box A to a word from Box B to make a word that matches each definition. You may use a dictionary to help you. The first one is done for you.

Box A	Box B
dis- mis-	spell agree behave like connected place
1. not like	*dislike*
2. spell incorrectly	_____
3. put in the wrong place	_____
4. act badly	_____
5. not plugged in	_____
6. not agree	_____

Review

disappear

misplace

- A **prefix** is a word part added at the beginning of a base word to change its meaning.
- The prefix *dis-* means "not" or "do the opposite of."
- The prefix *mis-* means "badly" or "incorrectly."

Sentence Solver

▶ Use the words you made in Match It to complete each sentence.

7. If I _____ the words on the pretest, I will need to study them some more.

8. The puppies _____ and chew on my slippers.

9. I always _____ my sneakers. I can never find them!

10. Yolanda and Sam do not get along. They _____ about everything.

11. I do not want to eat yams. I _____ them.

12. The computer is _____ right now.

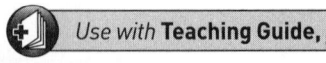

Use with **Teaching Guide,** *page 532.*

Word Parts

Suffixes
-tion, -sion

Name

Write It

► Write the base word for each word. The first one is done for you.

Word with Suffix	Base Word
1. celebration	*celebrate*
2. directions	
3. confusion	
4. decision	
5. information	
6. combination	
7. selection	
8. subtraction	

> ### Review
>
> celebration
>
> decision
>
> • A **suffix** is a word part added at the end of a base word to change its meaning.
> • The suffixes *-tion* and *-sion* change a word from a verb to a noun.

True or False

► Read each sentence. If it is true, circle *T*. If it is false, circle *F*. You may use a dictionary to help you. The first one is done for you.

9. **Rejection** is the acceptance of something.   T   Ⓕ

10. When you make a **selection**, you choose something.   T   F

11. When you make up your mind, you make a **decision**.   T   F

12. A **conclusion** is the start of something.   T   F

Use with **Teaching Guide,** *page 528.*

Word Parts

Suffixes
-able, -ible

Name _____

Build It

▶ Build new words by adding suffixes to the base words. Write each word on the line. You may use a dictionary to help you. **Hint:** You may need to drop the final *e* from some words before you add a suffix.

1. agree + able =

_____

2. sense + ible =

_____

3. comfort + able =

_____

4. collect + ible =

_____

5. read + able =

_____

6. reverse + ible =

_____

Write It

▶ Choose four words from Build It. Use each one in a sentence.

7. _____

8. _____

9. _____

10. _____

Add It

▶ Add *-able* or *-ible* to each underlined word. Then, write the new word on the line. Hint: You may need to drop the final *e* from some words before you add a suffix. The first one is done for you.

11. My new kitten is <u>adore</u>. _*adorable*_

12. This novel is very <u>enjoy</u>. _____

13. You need to be <u>flex</u> to do gymnastics. _____

14. The gold ring is <u>value</u>. _____

Word Parts

Prefixes
uni-, bi-, tri-

Name _____

Review

<u>uni</u>cycle

<u>bi</u>cycle

<u>tri</u>cycle

- A **prefix** is a word part added at the beginning of a base word to change its meaning.
- The prefix *uni-* means "one."
- The prefix *bi-* means "two."
- The prefix *tri-* means "three."

Circle It

▶ Circle the word in each row that has a prefix.

1. tripod   tangle   tricky

2. uncle   uniform   until

3. billed   boots   bifocals

4. trimming   triangle   thirsty

5. unicycle   under   until

6. basket   bike   biweekly

Sentence Solver

▶ Use words from the word bank to complete each sentence.

unite	bicycle	triplets	unicorn	triple	biceps

7. My two sisters and I are _____. We even look alike!

8. A storybook animal that looks like a horse with a horn is

   a _____.

9. I am exercising so my arms will have strong _____.

10. Miguel rides a _____ to class.

11. We will _____ to make one winning team.

12. Jess made a _____ play. She got three players out!

Use with **Teaching Guide,** *page 532.*

Name

Series 24 Review

24.1	midnight, subzero
24.2	disappear, misplace
24.3	celebration, decision
24.4	enjoyable, sensible
24.5	unicycle, bicycle, tricycle

Word List

▶ Read the words from left to right. The words are new, but you have the skills to read them. Circle the words that have the suffix **-tion**. Underline the word that has the suffix **-sion**.

action   addition   applications   debatable   discontent
disgraceful   explosion   unity   unreadable   subtitle

Define It

▶ Choose four words from the word bank. Find the meaning of the words in a dictionary. Write the definitions.

1._____

2._____

3._____

4._____

Build It

▶ Follow the directions to build new words. Write each word on the line.

5. Start with the word **grace.**
Add the suffix **-ful.**

_____

Now add the prefix **dis-.**

_____

6. Start with the word **use.**
Add the prefix **mis-**

_____

Now add the suffix **-ed.**

_____

Use with **Teaching Guide,** page 542.

Roots *bio, graph, auto*

Name _____

Sentence Solver

▶ Use words from the word bank to complete each sentence.

autographs	biography	graphics
biology	photographs	

Review

- **Roots** are parts of English words that come from other languages such as Latin and Greek.
- The Greek root *bio* means "life."
- The Greek root *graph* means "something written or drawn."
- The Greek root *auto* means "self."

1. We learn about nature in _____ class.

2. Treena likes to take _____ with her camera.

3. My favorite baseball players signed their _____ on my mitt.

4. I am reading a _____ about Ben Franklin.

5. Luís used charts and other _____ in his report.

Sort It

▶ Write each word from the word bank in the correct column of the chart. **Hint:** Some words may go in more than one column.

automate	biologist	digraph	biography
autobiography	biographer	graphite	automatic

6. auto = "self"	7. bio = "life"	8. graph = "write" or "draw"

Use with **Teaching Guide,** *page 536.*

Roots *port, dict*

Name

Review

air*port*

pre*dict*

- **Roots** are parts of English words that come from other languages such as Latin and Greek.
- The Latin root *port* means "to carry."
- The Latin root *dict* means "to say."

All Mixed Up

▶ Unscramble each word from the word bank to complete the sentences.

verdict	porter	seaport
portable	airport	dictating

1. Our plane landed at the _____. **partiro**

2. The crowd waited for the judge's _____. **reditcv**

3. Ms. Ruiz was _____ the words for the spelling test. **natitigcd**

4. At the hotel, a _____ carried our bags for us. **retorp**

5. The tiny phone is very _____. **belopart**

6. Many ships dock at our city's _____. **repoats**

Circle It

▶ Read each word. Circle each word that has the Latin roots *port* or *dict*. Then, underline the root.

7. export   enter   poster

8. present   predict   edit

9. inform   inventor   import

10. contact   contradict   decade

Write It

▶ Choose two of the words you circled in Circle It. Use each one in a sentence.

11. _____

12. _____

 Use with **Teaching Guide,** *page 536.*

Roots *rupt, struct, scrib/script*

Name

Sentence Solver

▶ Use words from the word bank to complete each sentence. There will be two words left over.

describes	eruption	instructions	manuscript
prescribe	reconstruct	scribble	subscribe

1. The volcano had a large _____.

2. The author finished her _____ and sent it to the publisher.

3. The teacher will give us _____ on how to take the test.

4. My doctor will _____ medicine.

5. Dani wants to _____ to a sports magazine.

6. When I write quickly, it looks like a _____.

Review

erupts

construct

scribble

manuscript

- **Roots** are parts of English words that come from other languages such as Latin and Greek.
- The Latin root *rupt* means "to break."
- The Latin root *struct* means "to build."
- The Latin roots *scrib* and *script* mean "to write."

Define It

▶ Read each word. Write the meaning of each word on the line next to it. You may use a dictionary to help you.

7. interrupt _____

8. obstruct _____

9. manuscript _____

10. reconstruct _____

Use with **Teaching Guide,** *page 536.*

Roots *scope*, *tele*, *phon*, *vis/vid*

Name _____

Find It

▶ **A.** Use words from the word bank to answer each clue. After you use a word, cross it out in the word bank.

evidence	invisible	microscope	revisited
saxophone	telephone	television	visible
phonics	microphone	telescope	visitors

1. This means "visited again." _____

2. This means "able to be seen." _____

3. Scientists use this to help them see tiny objects.

_____

4. This means "proof." _____

5. This is a musical instrument. _____

6. This means "cannot be seen." _____

7. This means "people who go to see something or someone."

_____

8. This is used to see objects that are far away. _____

9. This is the study of sounds and how they are spelled. _____

10. This can be used to make your voice louder. _____

11. This is used to make calls to other people. _____

▶ **B.** Write the word that is left in the word bank to answer this clue.

This invention was introduced at the 1939 World's Fair.

12. _____

Review

<u>micro**scope**</u>

<u>**tele**vise</u>

<u>saxo**phon**e</u>

<u>**vis**ible</u>

<u>e**vid**ence</u>

- **Roots** are parts of English words that come from other languages such as Latin and Greek.
- The Greek root ***scope*** means "to watch" or "look at."
- The Greek root ***tele*** means "far off" or "distant."
- The Greek root ***phon*** means "sound" or "voice."
- The Latin roots ***vis*** and ***vid*** mean "to see."

*Use with **Teaching Guide**, page 536.*

Word List

▶ Read the words from left to right. The words are new, but you have the skills to read them. Circle the word with the root **bio**. Underline the words with the root **script**.

> disrupt   earphones   geography   graphically   imported
>
> inscription   prescription   transcript   vista   biographies

Series 25 Review	
25.1	automatic, biology, graphics
25.2	airport, predict
25.3	erupts, construct, scribble, manuscript
25.4	microscope, televise, saxophone, visible, evidence

Find It

▶ Underline the words in each row that have one of the Greek or Latin roots in the box. Then, circle the root.
Hint: Some words may have more than one root.

> | auto | bio | graph | port | dict | struct |
> |---|---|---|---|---|---|
> | scrib | scope | tele | vis | phon | |

1. contradict   caution   obstruct

2. midnight   autographs   prescribe

3. megaphone   newspaper   televise

4. outlook   microscope   exported

5. biographer   flawless   visible

Just for Fun

▶ Say this tongue twister five times fast!

6. Scribblers scribble scribbled scripts.

Use with **Teaching Guide,** page 542.

Glossary of *System 44* Terms

▶ A glossary explains the meaning of terms, or special words. Use this glossary to find the meanings of terms used in *System 44* instruction.

adjective

A word that describes a noun or pronoun. For example, in the following sentence, *cold* is an adjective. It describes the drink. *The **cold** drink has lots of ice.*

adverb

A word usually used to describe a verb or an adjective. For example, in the following sentence, *quickly* is an adverb that tells *how* the girl ran. *The girl ran **quickly**.*

alphabet

All the letters of a written language arranged in order. *There are 26 letters in the English **alphabet**.*

base change

The spelling of some base words changes when an ending or suffix is added. Three types of base change are: (1) consonant doubling as in *run/running,* (2) drop final *e* as in *bake/baking,* and (3) change *y* to *i* as in *happy/happiness.*

base word

The form of a word with no prefixes, suffixes, or endings. For example, in the word *replayed, play* is the base word.

closed syllable

A syllable that ends in one or more consonants. It usually has a short vowel sound. Examples: *hab • it, pic • nic, plas • tic, rap • id*

consonant

Letters *b, c, d, f, g, h, j, k, l, m, n, p, q, r, s, t, v, w, x, y, z* are **consonants**. Letters *w* and *y* can also be vowels.

consonant blend

Two or more consonant letters that go together, and each one must be sounded. Examples: *spin, split, trap, black, fast, sand, dump*

consonant + -le, -el, -al syllables

When *-le, -el,* or *-al* appears at the end of a word, it usually represents the sound "ul." When breaking a word into syllables, keep these letters together with the consonant they follow. Examples: *ti • tle, grum • ble, la • bel, fi • nal*

contraction

A shortened combination of two words. The missing letters are represented with an apostrophe. Examples: *cannot/can't, she is/she's, I have/I've*

CVC (consonant-vowel-consonant)

The consonant-vowel-consonant, or CVC, spelling pattern usually signals that a vowel sound will be short. For example, these words have a CVC pattern: *can, sit, met, hot, nut.*

digraph

Two consonant letters that, when paired, stand for a single consonant sound. Examples: *ship, fish, chat, lunch, think, this, math, thing*

diphthong

A "gliding" vowel sound. Your mouth glides from one vowel sound to another when you say these sounds. Examples: *coin, toy, cloud, owl*

ending

An ending that is added to a base word. Endings may be added to nouns to show more than one (plurals). Examples: *cat/cats, wish/wishes.* Endings may be added to verbs to make them agree with the subject of the sentence. Example: *I miss you./She misses you.* Endings may also be added to verbs to indicate the time of the action. Example: *I will jump./I am jumping./I jumped.* The formal name for endings is *inflections.*

future tense

Verb form that tells that something is going to happen but has not happened yet. Example: *He **will bike** to school tomorrow.*

gliding sound

A gliding sound is made when your mouth moves smoothly from one vowel sound to another. Examples: *c<u>oi</u>n, t<u>oy</u>, cl<u>ou</u>d, <u>ow</u>l*. The formal name is *diphthong*.

long vowel sound

A vowel sound that is the same as the letter's name in the alphabet. Example: The vowel sounds in these words are long: *d<u>ay</u>, r<u>ai</u>n, f<u>ee</u>t, b<u>ea</u>n, b<u>i</u>ke, n<u>igh</u>t, c<u>oa</u>t, sn<u>ow</u>, c<u>u</u>te, fl<u>y</u>.*

noun

Any word is a noun if it can be the subject of a sentence. Most nouns are words that name a person, place, or thing. Examples: *The <u>boy</u> runs. The <u>ball</u> is blue. The <u>city</u> is busy.*

open syllable

A syllable that ends in a vowel and usually has a long vowel sound. Examples: *b<u>a</u> • sic, d<u>e</u> • cent, s<u>i</u> • lent, r<u>o</u> • bots, h<u>u</u> • man*

past tense

Verb form that tells that something already happened. Example: *The plane **landed** yesterday.*

prefix

A word part added at the beginning of a base word to change its meaning.

Prefixes		
Prefix	Meaning	Example
un-	not or opposite of	unlock
non-	not or opposite of	nonslip
de-	opposite of	defrost
com-	with	combine
con-	with	consist
re-	again	rewrite
pre-	before	pretest
mid-	in the middle of	midtown
sub-	below	subset
dis-	not or do the opposite of	disagree
mis-	badly or incorrectly	misspell
uni-	one	unicycle
bi-	two	bicycle
tri-	three	tricycle

present tense

Verb form that tells something that is happening now. *I am **meeting** her now.*

r-controlled vowel sound

When the letter *r* follows a vowel, the *r* can change the sound the vowel stands for. Examples: *sh<u>ar</u>k, g<u>er</u>m, b<u>ir</u>d*

r-controlled vowel sound syllable

A syllable that includes the letter *r* following a vowel. Examples: *<u>ar</u> • tist, p<u>ar</u> • ty*

root

Part of an English word that comes from other languages such as Latin or Greek.

Roots		
Root	Meaning	Example
bio	life	biography
graph	something written or drawn	graphics
auto	self	autobiography
port	carry	portable
dict	to say	dictate
rupt	break	erupts
struct	build	construct
scrib/ script	write	scribble
scope	to watch or look at	microscope
tele	far off	television
phon	sound or voice	telephone
vis/vid	to see	visible

schwa

The vowel sound in an unstressed syllable that is reduced or clipped when we say it. The schwa sound is similar to the short *u* sound. Examples: *ped<u>a</u>l, cam<u>e</u>l, tons<u>i</u>l, lem<u>o</u>n, cact<u>u</u>s*

short vowel sound

The type of sound the vowel stands for in words such as m<u>a</u>n, p<u>e</u>n, rip, h<u>o</u>t, and <u>u</u>p.

sight word

A word you see often in your reading that does not always follow a regular spelling pattern. Examples: *the, to, have, one, said*

silent consonant

Some letters in consonant pairs are not sounded when you say them but need to appear when you write them. Examples: *<u>k</u>not, lam<u>b</u>, <u>w</u>rite*

stressed syllable

A syllable that is pronounced with more emphasis than another. Examples: *<u>cam</u> • el, <u>in</u> • fant, <u>ped</u> • al, <u>chick</u> • en, ex • <u>cept</u>, re • <u>ply</u>*

suffix

A word part added at the end of a base word to change its meaning or part of speech.

Suffixes		
Suffix	**Meaning**	**Example**
-ment	state or condition	*content-ment*
-ness	state or condition	*stillness*
-y	being, having, able to	*lucky*
-ly	like or in a ____ way	*safely*
-er	one who does something	*teacher*
-or	one who does something	*actor*
-er	compares two people or things	*quicker*
-est	compares more than two people or things	*quickest*
-less	without	*spotless*
-ful	causing or full of	*cheerful*
-tion	the state of	*celebra-tion*
-sion	the state of	*decision*
-able	is or can be	*adorable*
-ible	is or can be	*reversible*

syllable

A unit of sound in a word. A syllable contains one vowel sound and may contain one or more consonants.

Syllables	
Number of Syllables	**Example**
one syllable	*bat*
two syllables	*jumping*
three syllables	*recommend*
four syllables	*undefeated*

unstressed syllable

A syllable that is pronounced with less emphasis than another. The vowel sound in an unstressed syllable may be reduced to the schwa sound.

VCe (vowel-consonant-e)

This spelling pattern usually signals that a vowel sound will be long. Examples: *c<u>a</u>pe, k<u>i</u>te, h<u>o</u>pe, c<u>u</u>be*

VCe (vowel-consonant-e) syllable

A syllable with the vowel-consonant-e pattern. This spelling pattern usually signals that a vowel sound in a syllable will be long. Examples: *re • l<u>a</u>te, in • v<u>i</u>te*

verb

A word that tells what the subject of a sentence is doing. Examples: *The girl jogs. The sun shines. The dog eats dog food.*

vowel sound

A speech sound made with a free flow of air through the mouth. Vowels are spelled with the letters *a, e, i, o, u* and sometimes *y* and *w.*

vowel spot

The letter or letters that spell the vowel sound in a syllable. Vowel spots may consist of one or more letters. Examples: *hat, soap, container, chimpanzees*

vowel team

Two vowel letters that stand for one vowel sound. Examples: *train, play, team, feet, shield, soap, snow*

vowel team syllable

A syllable in which two vowel letters stand for one vowel sound. Examples: *con • tain, es • say, free • dom, rea • son, rail • road, shad • ow*

word family

Words that have the same base or root are in the same word family. Examples: *construct, construction, reconstruct, constructs, constructed, constructing*

System 44 Log

▶ Use these pages to keep track of the Series you have completed. Check off each Topic you finish.

SERIES 1

- [ ] **1.1** Consonants *m, s*
- [ ] **1.2** Consonants *t, n*
- [ ] **1.3** Short *a*
- [ ] **1.4** Consonants *p, c*
- [ ] **1.5** Consonants *b, r*
- [ ] **1.6** Sight Words
- [ ] **1.7** Ending *-s*
- [ ] **1.8** Success

Bats Do That?

Rate this video

☆ ☆ ☆ ☆

00:00

SERIES 2

- [ ] **2.1** Short *i*
- [ ] **2.2** Consonants *d, f*
- [ ] **2.3** Consonants *h, k*
- [ ] **2.4** Short *o*
- [ ] **2.5** Consonants *l, x*
- [ ] **2.6** *-ck*
- [ ] **2.7** Sight Words
- [ ] **2.8** Success

Art for Kicks

Rate this video

☆ ☆ ☆ ☆

00:00

SERIES 3

- [ ] **3.1** s-Blends
- [ ] **3.2** Short *e*
- [ ] **3.3** Consonants *j, w*
- [ ] **3.4** Short *u*
- [ ] **3.5** Consonants *g, y*
- [ ] **3.6** Consonants *v, q, z*
- [ ] **3.7** Sight Words
- [ ] **3.8** Success

Run, Jesse, Run!

Rate this video

☆ ☆ ☆ ☆

00:00

SERIES 4

- [ ] **4.1** More s- Blends
- [ ] **4.2** Double Consonants
- [ ] **4.3** Final Blends
- [ ] **4.4** Identifying Syllables
- [ ] **4.5** Sight Words
- [ ] **4.6** Success

Passing the Sniff Test

Rate this video

☆ ☆ ☆ ☆

00:00

SERIES 5

- [ ] **5.1** l- Blends
- [ ] **5.2** r- Blends
- [ ] **5.3** More l- and r- Blends
- [ ] **5.4** Two- and Three-Letter Blends
- [ ] **5.5** Sight Words
- [ ] **5.6** Success

Brain Freeze

Rate this video

☆ ☆ ☆ ☆

00:00

Ivan

SYSTEM 44

SERIES 6

- [ ] **6.1** More Final Blends
- [ ] **6.2** -ng, -nk
- [ ] **6.3** Closed Syllables
- [ ] **6.4** -nt, -nd
- [ ] **6.5** Sight Words
- [ ] **6.6** Success

King of the Court

Rate this video

☆ ☆ ☆ ☆

SERIES 7

- [ ] **7.1** Digraph *sh*
- [ ] **7.2** Digraph *ch*
- [ ] **7.3** *ch*, -tch
- [ ] **7.4** *sh*, *ch*, -tch
- [ ] **7.5** Ending -es
- [ ] **7.6** Sight Words
- [ ] **7.7** Success

Something Fishy

Rate this video

☆ ☆ ☆ ☆

SERIES 8

- [ ] **8.1** Digraph *th*
- [ ] **8.2** Digraph Review
- [ ] **8.3** Ending -ing
- [ ] **8.4** Ending -ed
- [ ] **8.5** More on Ending -ed
- [ ] **8.6** Endings -ing, -ed
- [ ] **8.7** Sight Words
- [ ] **8.8** Success

High-Flying Circus

Rate this video

☆ ☆ ☆ ☆

SERIES 9

- [ ] **9.1** Unstressed Closed Syllables *(a, e)*
- [ ] **9.2** Unstressed Closed Syllables *(i, o, u)*
- [ ] **9.3** Consonant + -le
- [ ] **9.4** Consonant + -al, -el
- [ ] **9.5** Sight Words
- [ ] **9.6** Success

Struggle for Survival

Rate this video

☆ ☆ ☆ ☆

SERIES 10

- [ ] **10.1** Long *a (a_e)*
- [ ] **10.2** Long *i (i_e)*
- [ ] **10.3** Long *a, i (VCe)*
- [ ] **10.4** Soft *c*
- [ ] **10.5** Soft *g*
- [ ] **10.6** Suffixes -ment, -ness
- [ ] **10.7** Sight Words
- [ ] **10.8** Success

Live from the Hive

Rate this video

☆ ☆ ☆ ☆

Erica

System 44 Log continued

▶ Use these pages to keep track of the Series you have completed. Check off each Topic you finish.

SERIES 11

- ☐ **11.1** Long o (o_e)
- ☐ **11.2** Long u (u_e)
- ☐ **11.3** VCe Syllables
- ☐ **11.4** More VCe Syllables
- ☐ **11.5** Prefixes un-, non-, de-
- ☐ **11.6** Sight Words
- ☐ **11.7** Success

Hero of Hope
Rate this video
☆ ☆ ☆ ☆

SERIES 12

- ☐ **12.1** Ending -ing (drop e)
- ☐ **12.2** Ending -ing (with doubling)
- ☐ **12.3** Ending -ed (drop e)
- ☐ **12.4** Ending -ed (with doubling)
- ☐ **12.5** Sight Words
- ☐ **12.6** Success

Up and Running
Rate this video
☆ ☆ ☆ ☆

SERIES 13

- ☐ **13.1** y as a Vowel
- ☐ **13.2** Suffixes -y, -ly
- ☐ **13.3** Changing -y to i
- ☐ **13.4** Digraphs wh, ph
- ☐ **13.5** Sight Words
- ☐ **13.6** Success

Flies that Spy
Rate this video
☆ ☆ ☆ ☆

SERIES 14

- ☐ **14.1** Silent Consonants
- ☐ **14.2** Open Syllables
- ☐ **14.3** More Open Syllables
- ☐ **14.4** Unstressed Open Syllables
- ☐ **14.5** Prefixes con-, com-
- ☐ **14.6** Sight Words
- ☐ **14.7** Success

Robots: Now It's Personal
Rate this video
☆ ☆ ☆ ☆

SERIES 15

- ☐ **15.1** Long a (ai)
- ☐ **15.2** Long a (ay)
- ☐ **15.3** Long a Vowel Team Syllables
- ☐ **15.4** Sight Words
- ☐ **15.5** Success

Hail to the Chef
Rate this video
☆ ☆ ☆ ☆

SERIES 16

- ☐ **16.1** Long *o* (*oa*)
- ☐ **16.2** Long *o* (*ow*)
- ☐ **16.3** Long *o* Vowel Team Syllables
- ☐ **16.4** Sight Words
- ☐ **16.5** Success

Going Coastal

Rate this video

☆ ☆ ☆ ☆

SERIES 17

- ☐ **17.1** Prefixes *re-, pre-*
- ☐ **17.2** Long *e* (*ea*)
- ☐ **17.3** Long *e* (*ee*)
- ☐ **17.4** Long *e* (*ie*)
- ☐ **17.5** Long *e* Vowel Team Syllables
- ☐ **17.6** Sight Words
- ☐ **17.7** Success

The Dream Team

Rate this video

☆ ☆ ☆ ☆

SERIES 18

- ☐ **18.1** Long *i* (-*igh*)
- ☐ **18.2** Other Long Vowel Spellings
- ☐ **18.3** Analyzing Word Structure
- ☐ **18.4** Sight Words
- ☐ **18.5** Success

Get Ready to Roll!

Rate this video

☆ ☆ ☆ ☆

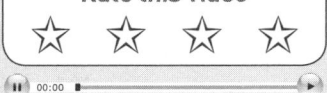

SERIES 19

- ☐ **19.1** *ar*
- ☐ **19.2** Syllables with *ar*
- ☐ **19.3** *er, ir, ur*
- ☐ **19.4** Syllables with *er, ir, ur*
- ☐ **19.5** Other /sh/ Spellings
- ☐ **19.6** Sight Words
- ☐ **19.7** Success

Shark Attack?

Rate this video

☆ ☆ ☆ ☆

SERIES 20

- ☐ **20.1** *or, ore*
- ☐ **20.2** Syllables with *or, ore*
- ☐ **20.3** Suffixes -*er*, -*or*
- ☐ **20.4** Suffixes -*er*, -*est*
- ☐ **20.5** *air* (hair), *are* (scare), *ear* (bear)
- ☐ **20.6** Syllables with /air/
- ☐ **20.7** Success

A Born Winner

Rate this video

☆ ☆ ☆ ☆

Success ☀

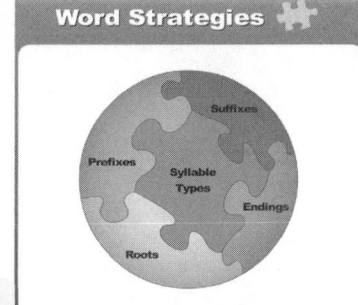

Word Strategies

Suffixes
Prefixes
Syllable Types
Endings
Roots

System 44 Log continued

▶ Use these pages to keep track of the Series you have completed. Check off each Topic you finish.

SERIES 21

- ☐ **21.1** *oi, oy*
- ☐ **21.2** Syllables with *oi, oy*
- ☐ **21.3** *ou* (*cloud*), *ow* (*owl*),
- ☐ **21.4** Syllables with *ou, ow*
- ☐ **21.5** Sight Words
- ☐ **21.6** Success

Get Down and Clown!

Rate this video

☆ ☆ ☆ ☆

SERIES 22

- ☐ **22.1** Suffixes *-less, -ful*
- ☐ **22.2** *oo* (*boot*), *ew* (*news*), *u_e* (*tube*)
- ☐ **22.3** Syllables with *oo, ew, u_e*
- ☐ **22.4** Sight Words
- ☐ **22.5** Success

Pit Crew U

Rate this video

☆ ☆ ☆ ☆

SERIES 23

- ☐ **23.1** *oo* (*book*), *u* (*put*)
- ☐ **23.2** Syllables with *oo, u*
- ☐ **23.3** *aw* (*paw*), *au* (*cause*), *a* (*ball*)
- ☐ **23.4** Syllables with *aw, au, a*
- ☐ **23.5** Success

Look Out Below!

Rate this video

☆ ☆ ☆ ☆

Mark

SERIES 24

- ☐ **24.1** Prefixes *mid-, sub-*
- ☐ **24.2** Prefixes *dis-, mis-*
- ☐ **24.3** Suffixes *-tion, -sion*
- ☐ **24.4** Suffixes *-able, -ible*
- ☐ **24.5** Prefixes *uni-, bi-, tri-*
- ☐ **24.6** Success

Back in Action

Rate this video

☆ ☆ ☆ ☆

SERIES 25

- ☐ **25.1** Roots *bio, graph, auto*
- ☐ **25.2** Roots *port, dict*
- ☐ **25.3** Roots *rupt, struct, scrib/script*
- ☐ **25.4** Roots *scope, tele, phon, vis/vid*
- ☐ **25.5** Success

Congratulations!

Rate this video

☆ ☆ ☆ ☆

System 44 Reading Log

Use these pages to keep track of the *System 44* Library books you read.

- Write the title in the book cover below. Add a design if you like.
- Fill in the date that you started and completed each book.
- Rate the book using the rating scale at right.
- Then, complete the statement about the book.

Rating Scale	
It was great!	★ ★ ★ ★
It was good!	★ ★ ★ ☆
It was O.K.	★ ★ ☆ ☆
I didn't like it.	★ ☆ ☆ ☆

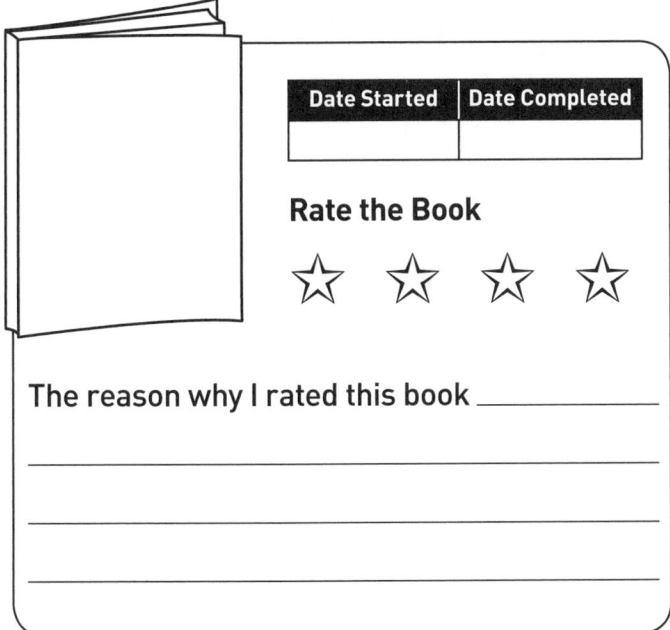

Date Started	Date Completed

Rate the Book

☆ ☆ ☆ ☆

The reason why I rated this book _____

_____

_____

_____

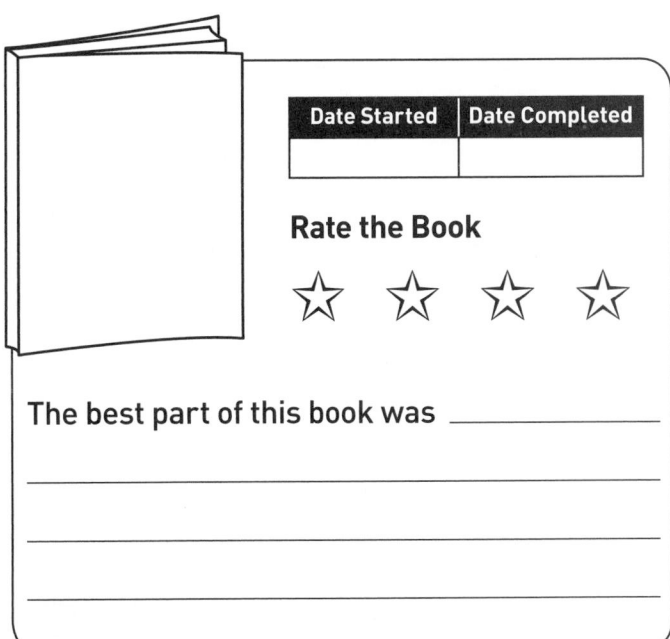

Date Started	Date Completed

Rate the Book

☆ ☆ ☆ ☆

The best part of this book was _____

_____

_____

_____

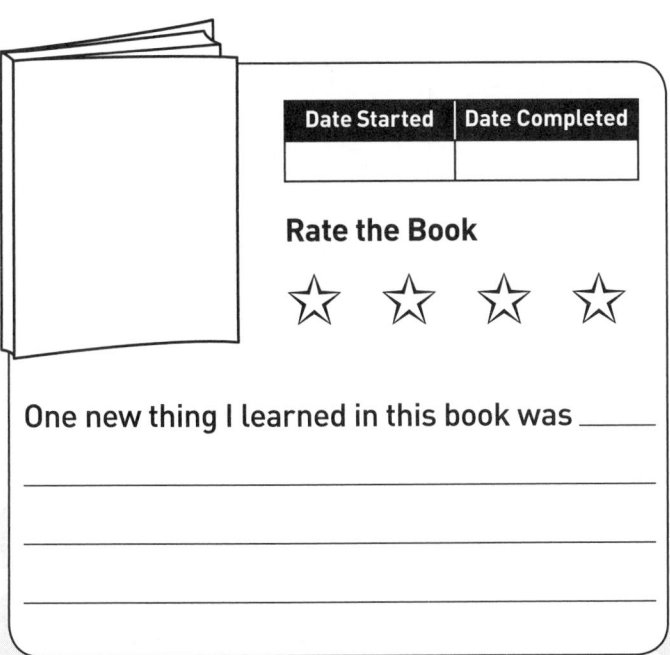

Date Started	Date Completed

Rate the Book

☆ ☆ ☆ ☆

One new thing I learned in this book was _____

_____

_____

_____

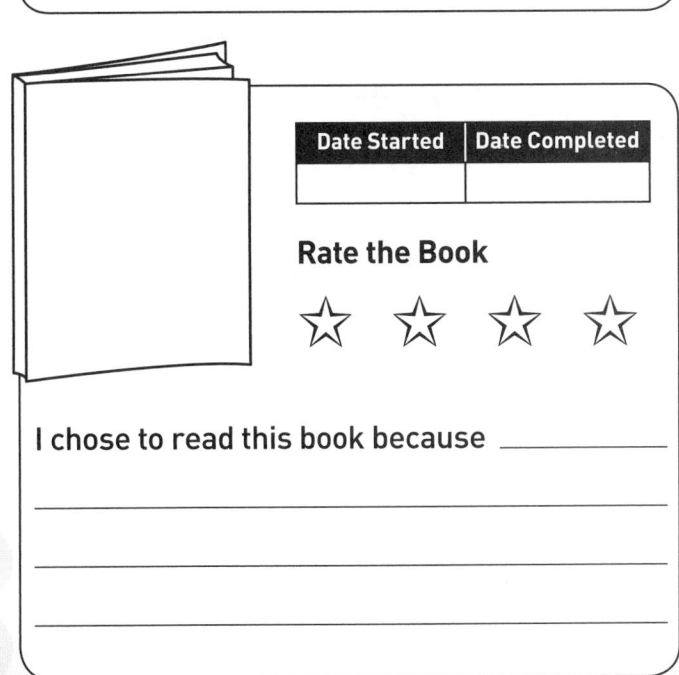

Date Started	Date Completed

Rate the Book

☆ ☆ ☆ ☆

I chose to read this book because _____

_____

_____

_____

System 44 Reading Log continued

Date Started	Date Completed

Rate the Book

☆ ☆ ☆ ☆

Three words that describe this book are _____

_____

_____

_____

_____

_____

Date Started	Date Completed

Rate the Book

☆ ☆ ☆ ☆

I chose to read this book because _____

_____

_____

_____

_____

_____

_____

Date Started	Date Completed

Rate the Book

☆ ☆ ☆ ☆

One fact I learned in this book is _____

_____

_____

_____

_____

_____

Date Started	Date Completed

Rate the Book

☆ ☆ ☆ ☆

When I first saw this book, I thought _____

_____

_____

_____

_____

_____

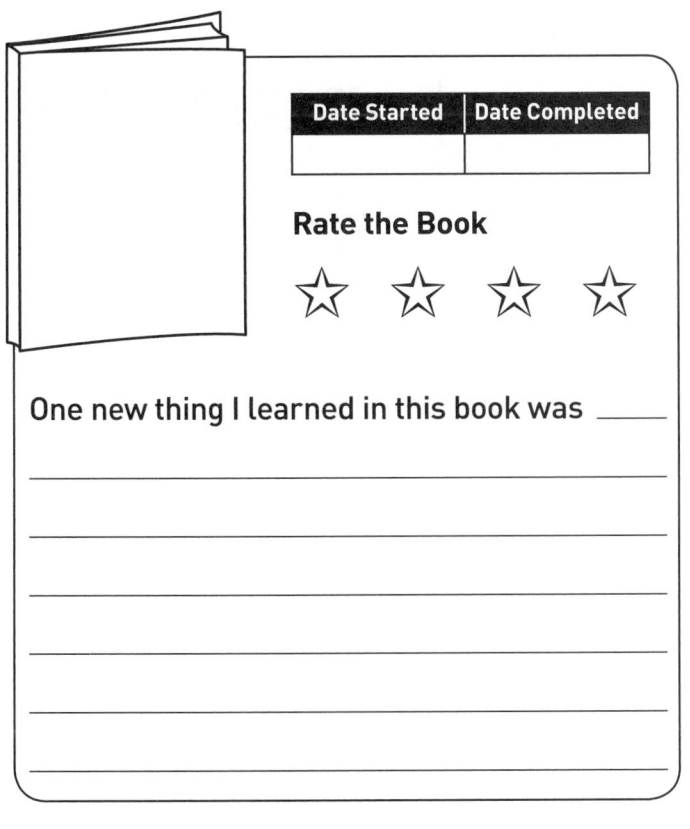

Date Started	Date Completed

Rate the Book

☆ ☆ ☆ ☆

One new thing I learned in this book was _____

_____

_____

_____

_____

_____

Date Started	Date Completed

Rate the Book

☆ ☆ ☆ ☆

One question I have for the author is _____

_____

_____

_____

_____

_____

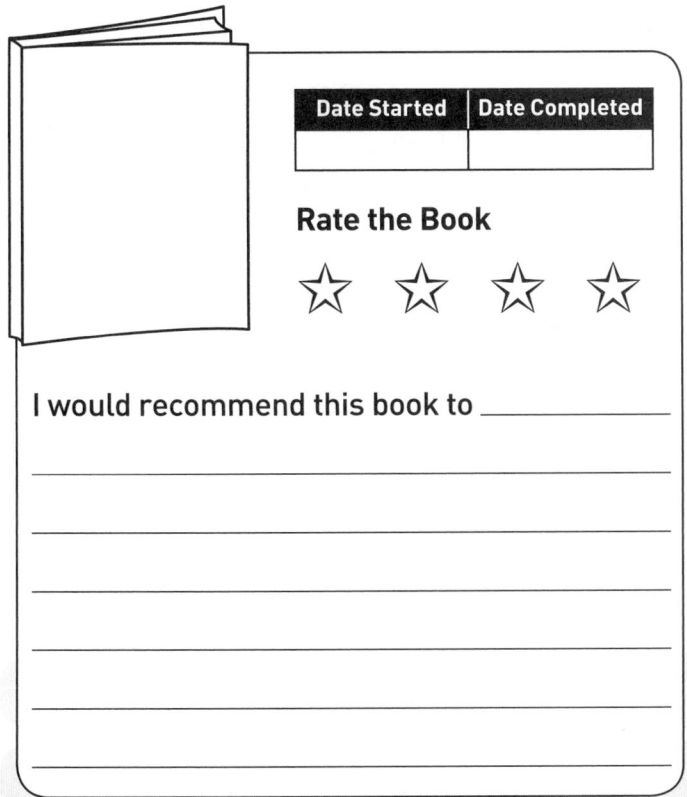

Date Started	Date Completed

Rate the Book

☆ ☆ ☆ ☆

I would recommend this book to _____

_____

_____

_____

_____

_____

Date Started	Date Completed

Rate the Book

☆ ☆ ☆ ☆

Reading this book made me feel _____

_____

_____

_____

_____

_____

System 44 Reading Log continued

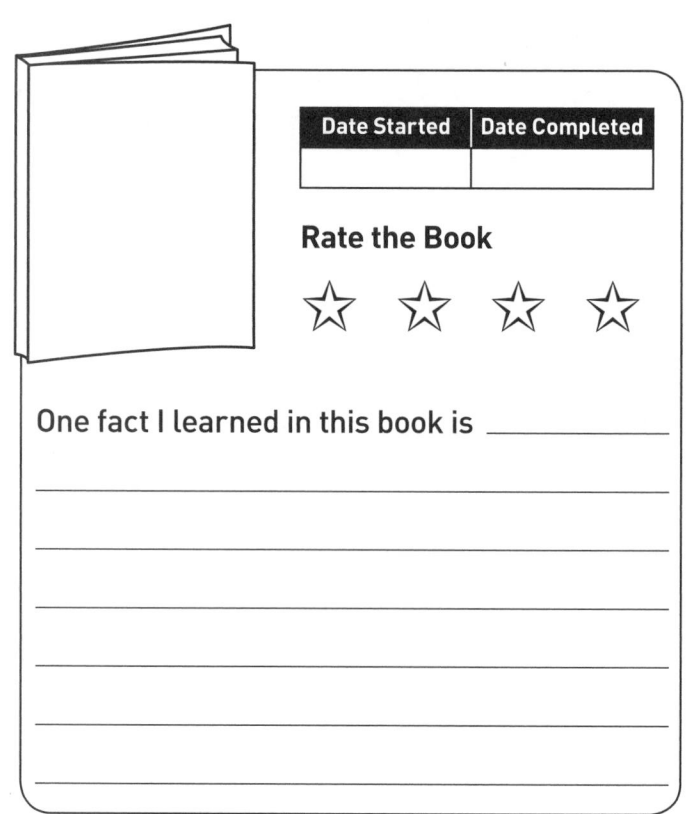

Date Started	Date Completed

Rate the Book

☆ ☆ ☆ ☆

One fact I learned in this book is _____

_____

_____

_____

_____

_____

Date Started	Date Completed

Rate the Book

☆ ☆ ☆ ☆

This book reminded me of _____

_____

_____

_____

_____

_____

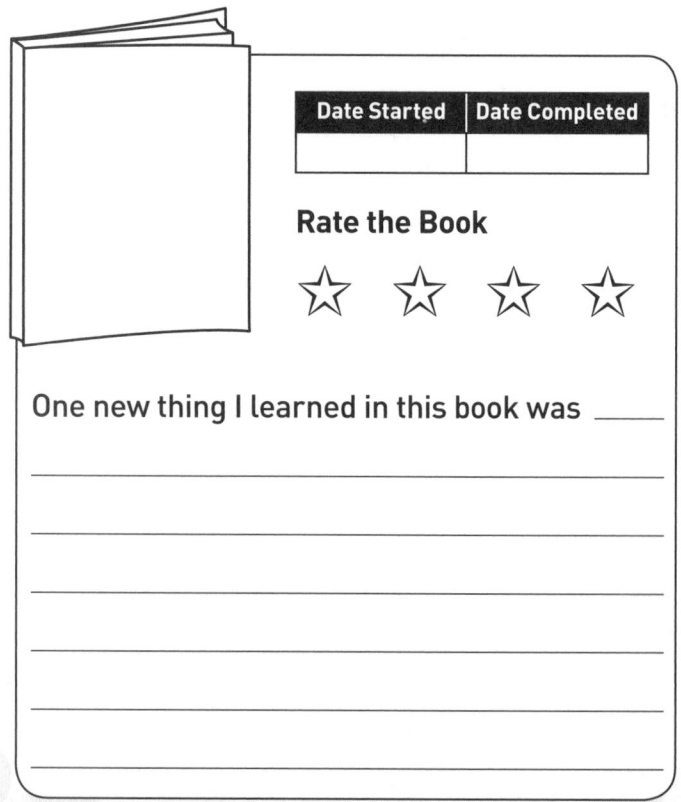

Date Started	Date Completed

Rate the Book

☆ ☆ ☆ ☆

One new thing I learned in this book was _____

_____

_____

_____

_____

_____

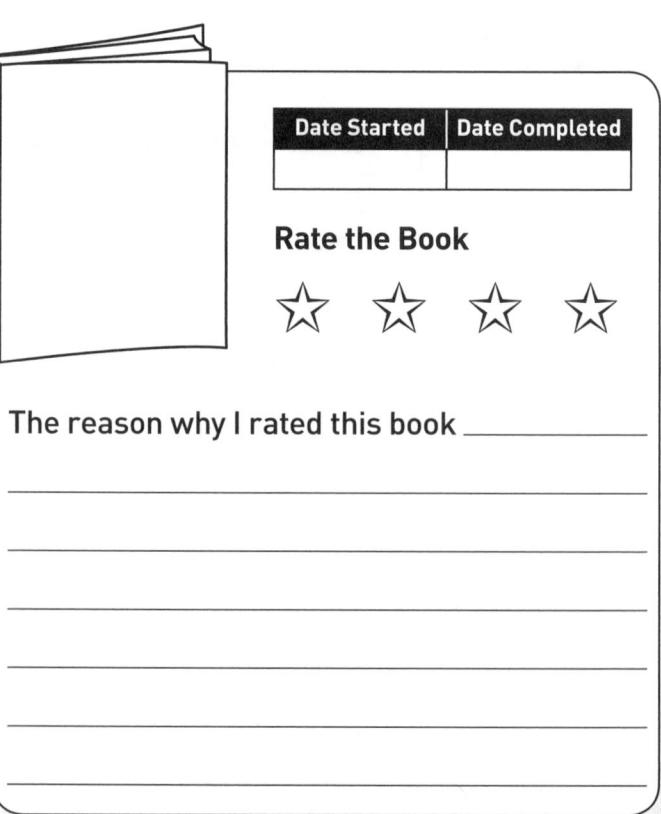

Date Started	Date Completed

Rate the Book

☆ ☆ ☆ ☆

The reason why I rated this book _____

_____

_____

_____

_____

_____

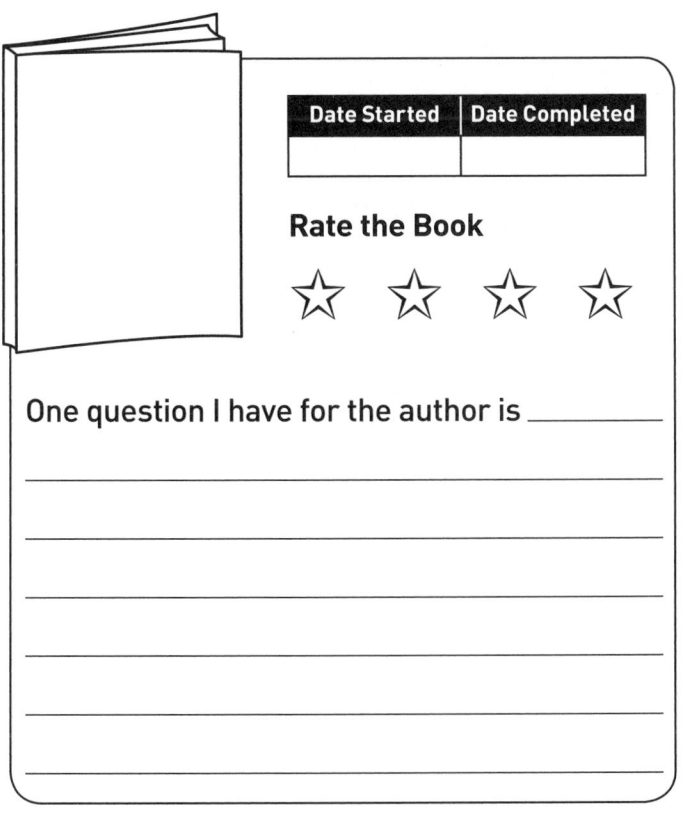

Date Started	Date Completed

Rate the Book

☆ ☆ ☆ ☆

One question I have for the author is _____

_____

_____

_____

_____

_____

Date Started	Date Completed

Rate the Book

☆ ☆ ☆ ☆

The best part of this book was _____

_____

_____

_____

_____

_____

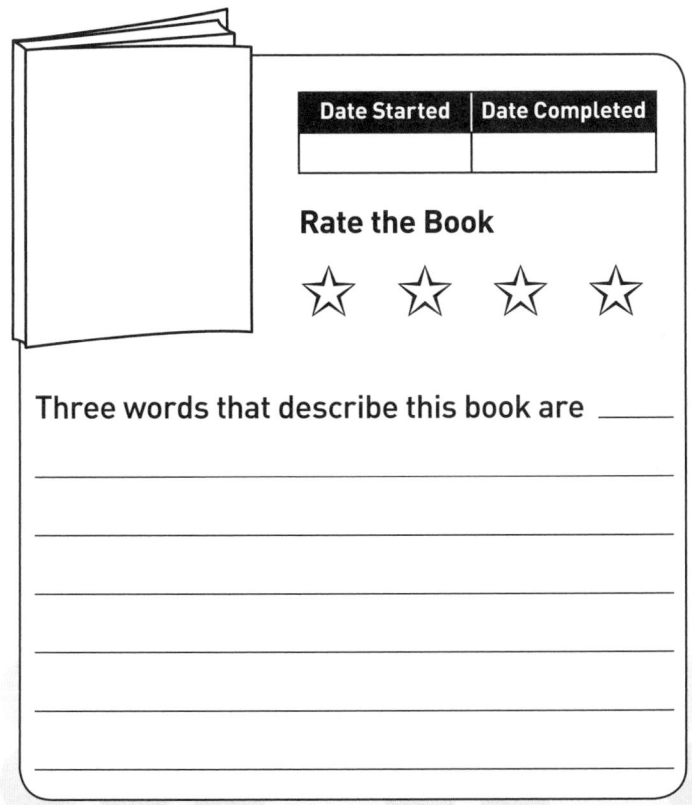

Date Started	Date Completed

Rate the Book

☆ ☆ ☆ ☆

Three words that describe this book are _____

_____

_____

_____

_____

_____

Date Started	Date Completed

Rate the Book

☆ ☆ ☆ ☆

I chose to read this book because _____

_____

_____

_____

_____

_____

Mouth Positions

Vowel Sounds Mouth Positions

e secret

i inch

a table

a apple

i pilot

o online

u up

aw yawn

o robot

oo book

oo moon

oi coin

ou cloud

er germ

ar cart

or sport

Consonant Sounds Mouth Positions

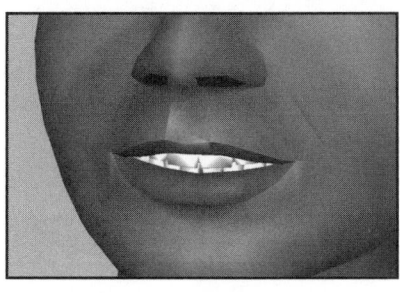

ⓣ **t**iger ⓝ **n**ose
ⓓ **d**og ⓛ **l**ips

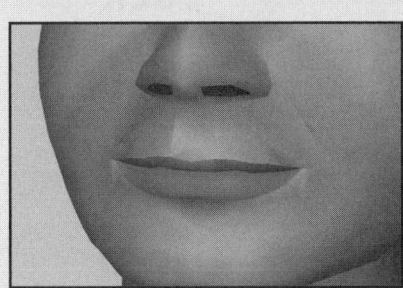

ⓟ **p**an ⓜ **m**ouse
ⓑ **b**at

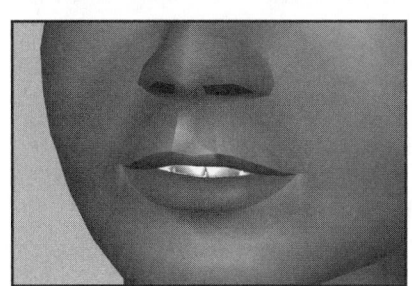

ⓒ **c**at
ⓖ **g**as

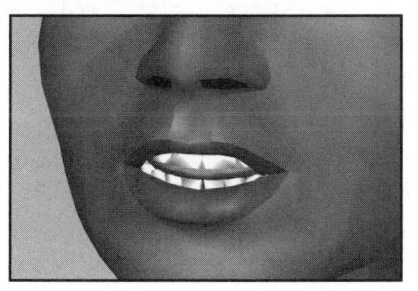

ⓣⓗ **th**ink

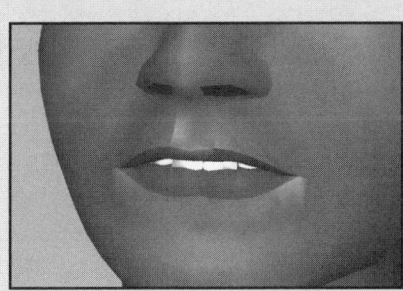

ⓕ **f**an
ⓥ **v**an

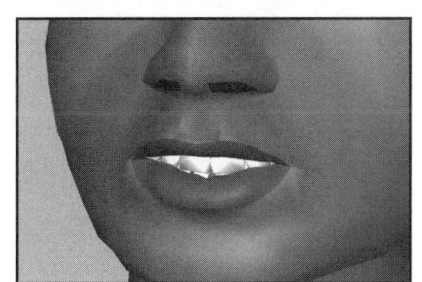

ⓒⓗ **ch**op ⓢⓗ **sh**ip
ⓙ **j**et

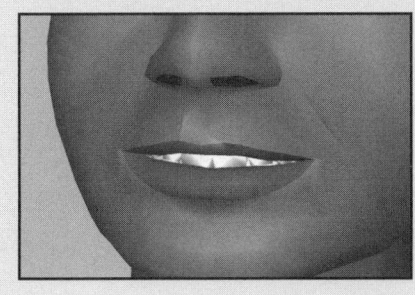

ⓢ **s**un
ⓩ **z**ip

Word Attack Strategy

1 **Look**

2 **Spot**

3 **Split**

4 **Read**

Using the Strategy

	Strategy Step	Examples	
1	**Look** for any prefixes, suffixes, or endings you know. • Remember, the spelling of the base word may have changed when the ending or suffix was added.	admitted admit(t) • <u>ed</u>	undefeated <u>un</u> • defeat • <u>ed</u>
2	**Spot** the vowels in the base word. The number of vowel spots tells the number of syllables. • Remember, some vowel sounds are spelled with more than one letter.	**a**dm**i**t(t) • ed	un • d**e**f**ea**t • ed
3	**Split** the word into syllables. • A good place to split a word is between two consonants. • If there is only one consonant between syllables, try splitting after it. • If the word doesn't sound right, try moving the split backward or forward by one letter.	a<u>d</u> • <u>m</u>it(t) • ed	~~un • def • eat • ed~~ un • d<u>e</u> • f<u>ea</u>t • ed
4	**Read** the word. Does it make a real word? If it does not, try again. • You may need to experiment with pronouncing the vowel sound differently.	admitted	undefeated

Six Syllable Types

 Closed Syllable

A closed syllable ends in a consonant. It usually has a short vowel sound.

   a. **hun • dred**

   b. **fan • tas • tic**

   c. **traf • fic**

 Consonant + -le, -el, or -al

The consonant + -le, -el, or -al pattern usually forms its own syllable. You can split a word with the consonant + -le, -el, or -al pattern before the consonant to make it easier to read.

   a. **an • gle**

   b. **tun • nel**

   c. **sig • nal**

 VCe Syllable

Syllables with the vowel-consonant-e pattern (VCe) have a long vowel sound. When you split a word with this pattern into syllables, keep the letters of the VCe pattern together.

   a. **on • line**

   b. **com • pute**

   c. **base • ment**

 Open Syllable

An open syllable ends in a vowel. It usually has a long vowel sound.

   a. **ca • ble**

   b. **le • gal**

   c. **mu • sic**

 Vowel Team Syllable

When you split a word with a vowel team, keep the letters of the vowel team in the same syllable.

   a. **con • tain**

   b. **rea • son**

   c. **dis • count**

   d. **free • dom**

 r-Controlled Vowel Syllable

When the letter r follows a vowel, the r can change the sound the vowel stands for.

   a. **a • part • ment**

   b. **per • son**

   c. **re • turn**

   d. **thirst • y**

Notes

Notes

Notes

Notes

Notes

Notes

Notes